FEED YOUR FAMILY

EXCITING NEW RECIPES TRIED AND TESTED BY 1000s OF KIDS

BY

**NICOLE PISANI
& JOANNA WEINBERG**

OF

CHEFS IN SCHOOLS

PAVILION

FOR OUR PARENTS, WHO FED US SO WELL

First published in the United Kingdom in 2022 by
Pavilion
43 Great Ormond Street
London
WC1N 3HZ

ISBN 978-1-91166-387-4

A CIP catalogue record for this book is available from the British Library.
10 9 8 7 6 5 4 3 2 1

Reproduction by Rival Colour Ltd., UK
Printed and bound by Toppan Printing Co., Ltd.
www.pavilionbooks.com

Photographer: Issy Croker
Food Stylists: Nicole Pisani and Emily Ezekiel
Commissioning editor: Sophie Allen
Design manager: Nicky Collings
Production manager: Phil Brown

CONTENTS

THE CHEFS IN SCHOOLS WAY

A group of 7-year-olds are gathered around what appears to be a plant pot at a table. You can see carrot tops growing out of it, and cucumber spears buried in what looks like rich, dark, crumbly soil. The kids are poking at it, curious – there's clearly some kind of game or dare going on. Alex pulls out a carrot, looks at the others and takes a bite, chews, then swallows it, looking pleased with himself. The group squeals. It's Mina's turn to go next. She takes her bite, then spits it out, and they all fall about laughing. The others pile in and have a go. The volume of their chatter goes up as they pull the vegetables out of their 'soil' – in this case, hummus topped with spiced, dried black olives and toasted breadcrumbs.

This is school lunch – the Chefs in Schools way.

Every day, children in our schools come into the dining hall to find sharing platters on the tables for them to explore. Some days, this will be tender whole cauliflowers, roasted until golden in star anise, with a knife sticking out of them for the children to carve up themselves. On others, it might be earthy, garlicky falafel to dip into yogurt, or vegetable sushi rolls.

After this will come the hot main course – sometimes inspired by dishes from the restaurant experience of our head chefs (such as the Edible Garden from Nopi that David made for his large secondary school in Hounslow), but just as often

FOR PRODUCE THAT IS BETTER FOR YOU AND THE PLANET — START WITH SEASONALITY.

Go online

USE THE CODE: INSEASON

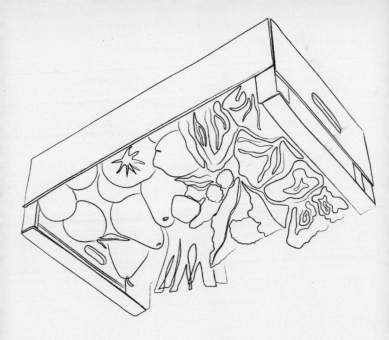

seasonal produce at
natoora.com

TAKE 20% OFF

they come from the home cooking of our school kitchen teams, such as Toni's Jollof Rice or SouSou's Burek.

We've had plenty of disasters, too. There was the lunch hour that our co-founder, Nicole, spent weeping over (and sweeping up) the 500 rejected portions of fresh mushroom tagliatelle she'd been making since 6 a.m. But that doesn't stop us being brave about our dishes, at least most of the time. Yes, we add a kick of chilli or a fragrant note of lemongrass because we believe that kids deserve to be offered food every bit as delicious as the variety that we adults get to make and eat.

Feeding kids every day is what we do. It is a rollercoaster: when a child picks up an asparagus spear and chomps the top off, or names a fresh herb, it's exhilarating. When they tip a perfectly executed 24-hour-braised lamb into the bin, or reject lovingly debearded mussels (seriously, imagine making enough to feed 500), we feel crushed. But we come back the next day and do it all again. We're dedicated to feeding kids. We know the risks and the rewards, and we love doing it. Most of all, for all the many reasons that you will discover through the course of this book, we think it's worth doing really well.

ABOUT THIS BOOK

Sometimes, at the school gate, a parent will collar one of the chefs and ask for a recipe that their child has mentioned. We've always tried to share whenever we can and yet receiving a piece of paper with notes and volumes to feed 500 isn't all that helpful. So we decided to collect some of our favourite – and most successful – recipes into a book. After all, why should the fun be limited to school? And we've also included family recipes from some of our greatest supporters in the food world, like Yotam Ottolenghi, Thomasina Miers, Anna Jones and Henry Dimbleby.

Yes, cooking at home for our families is a different world to producing the large quantities of food needed for a school meal. But the spirit is just the same. A shared meal, made from fresh ingredients does take time, and might not always be appreciated. However, it can also be the most rewarding, memorable and joyful thing you can do for, and enjoy with, your family. It's definitely worth a try.

This book is for anyone who wants to cook food from scratch for their families. Most of the recipes in it are simple enough for the novice cook to have a go at, yet there's also plenty to inspire a more accomplished cook. It includes a huge array of flavours and ingredients drawn from around the world for families who want to try something new. We truly hope that there is something in it for everyone.

To help you navigate, the book is divided into three parts. This first part, The Chefs in Schools Way, is an introduction to us, the way we work and what matters to us. Kitchen Smarts (p. 18) is a practical section to help you set up your kitchen stores, and to plan, shop and cook efficiently. Part three (p. 32) is where you'll find the flavour – our recipes.

BELOW, from left to right: Jake Barwood, Helen Cottle, Jacob Taylor, Yenny Chong, Oliver Pisani, Adam Bernstein, Sam Riches, Polly Praill, Nicole Pisani, Lidka D'Agostino, Danielle Glavin, Naomi Duncan, Henry Dimbleby, Louise Nichols, Joanna Weinberg, Saher Shah, Nerissa Buckley

NICOLE PISANI

"It all began in 2013 when I was Head Chef at Nopi, an Ottolenghi restaurant in central London. I had been rolling out high-end meals, such as Cod with Rassam and Pork Belly in Black Bean Sauce, for a privileged few for most of my working life. I was itching to tackle a new challenge when I saw a tweet from Henry Dimbleby (co-founder of Leon Restaurants and co-author of the School Food Plan), calling for an inspiring chef to turn around the food at his children's school in Hackney. I thought, Yes! – a chance to put my skills forward and inspire a new generation of eaters.

I took the job – and only after that, went in for lunch. It was my first 'school dinner'. I'm from Malta, where you go home for lunch every day. The first thing that struck me was the overcooked cabbage and a heavy, meaty smell that is so distinctive. The dining hall was noisy and stressful. Clearly some of the kids were frightened. The food was dolloped onto their plate and most of it went straight into the bin at the end of lunch. Going round the back, into the kitchen, explained so much. It was filled with ultra-processed foods that just needed heating up.

I was perplexed. When I was growing up in Malta, eating delicious, fresh food every day was as basic a human right as breathing and sleeping. Today, we live in a world obsessed with food. We Instagram every meal and have access to any kind of food we could wish for, during any season. I just couldn't believe that children were being asked to eat this version of 'food'. So, I took the job and set about creating change.

I wanted to blow the minds and taste buds of everyone at that school. I wanted to serve them juicy chicken, roasted in Moroccan spices, and colour their rice with turmeric. I wanted to place sharing platters of kisir, kimchi and pickles on the tables and let them explore for themselves. And I wanted to teach them to cook; to really cook – and not just cupcakes, but how to knead bread and blitz soup and how to butcher chickens and cook over fire."

Nicole didn't know it at the time but, at this one school in Hackney, with the support of a visionary Executive Head Teacher (Louise Nichols), Chefs in Schools was born.

Food in schools has come a long way over the past generation. Thanks to the light that Jamie Oliver and Jeanette Orrey shone on school dinners, there are next to no turkey twizzlers on the menu these days. The School Food Plan, led by Henry Dimbleby (now our Chair) and John Vincent in 2012 put new standards on the table, along with £580 million of government money, which provides free school meals for all children up to Year 2. However, the norm was still bland, boring and beige, and it wasn't good enough.

The School Food Plan team found plenty of schools doing food well, and discovered that there are as many different ways of doing good school food as there are schools themselves. In some, it's a community effort: parents and producers make a plan to grow, source and cook fresh food for their local school, while at others, contract caterers have committed to fresh produce and seasonally inspired menus.

The Chefs in Schools way is grounded in restaurant practice and we train up kitchen teams to have restaurant level skills. An important part of our mission is to instil pride in a workforce, made up predominantly of women, who do one of the most important jobs in our society: feed our children. All too often they are unrecognised and denied opportunities for professional development. Chefs trained by us can hold their own in a restaurant kitchen; they receive a School Chef qualification, demonstrating that they have the practical skills necessary to cook food that meets the School Food Standards and improve children's health. Through the training, they also develop skills in how to make learning about food fun for children and get them excited about trying new flavours and ingredients.

It's the Head Chef's job to work closely with suppliers – grocers, fishmongers, butchers – to source the best quality ingredients they can afford, enabling them to swap out the traditional school catering model of buying in as many dried and prepared ingredients in favour of fresh. These days, those freezers have become fridges, and they are filled with green broccoli, crisp lettuce and shiny tomatoes, marinating meat and whole sides of hake, straight from the sea.

MISSION

Our mission is to improve the health of children through better eating and food education.

Behind those very plain words sits a group of people – a movement, in fact, of chefs, teachers, campaigners and parents – who all believe passionately in the power of food to bring nourishment, nurture and sustenance to a new generation. We believe a school dinner is so much more than a filler to get a child through the school day – in many of our schools, lunch can be the only chance a child gets to eat.

Eating well at school helps both behaviour and attainment, which in turn are key to social mobility and children fulfilling their potential. While we have always believed school food to be a vitally important source of nutrients and sustenance for kids, Covid-19 concreted this as a fact for us.

BELOW, from left to right: Yenny Chong, Polly Praill, Danielle Glavin, Nicole Pisani, Naomi Duncan, Saher Shah

"Just before the first Covid lockdown in March 2020, two little girls came up to the pass. One of them was really shy and the other was holding her hand to encourage her. The shy girl asked for seconds. She was really hungry because there was no food at home and she wanted to take some home to her sister who had nothing to eat. I wrapped up a load of fish and beans so she could take them back at the end of the day, and I told the Headteacher. The school took care of that family's food for the whole of lockdown."
Nerissa, Chef Trainer

Never before have we needed food to do so much. Our country is facing a crisis in diet-related ill health, and children are at the forefront of it. These days, one in ten children arrives at primary school obese and, by the time they start secondary school, it is one in five. In areas with the highest levels of socio-economic deprivation, these statistics nearly double, to one in three. Research by the Food Foundation estimates that over 4 million children are living in poverty and these children face malnutrition as well as obesity, often at the same time.

In the end, it comes down to this: all children deserve to eat well and school is the one place where we can reach them.

ABOUT US AND WHAT WE DO

The challenge that we set ourselves when we launched in 2018 was, if we can make food as fresh and inspiring as a restaurant in one school, could we do it in a hundred? We gave ourselves five years to try.

We are a charity working to transform how food and food education is delivered in schools. We do that by helping schools implement the philosophy and method that Nicole developed in that first school kitchen she walked into. We train teams to run school kitchens with the passion for food and professionalism of a restaurant. We support schools to provide food lessons that inspire children, and we campaign tirelessly to make sure that as many children as possible can access great food in schools.

OUR FOOD

The chefs we work with cook food that is bright, colourful and culturally varied. Most importantly, it is packed with flavour. We don't dumb it down or believe that children will only eat very basic food. From delicately scented Keralan Fish Moilee Curry to Corn Ribs, this is the food that you will find in the pages of this book. Some of it comes from our experience as restaurant chefs, and much of it comes from the different cultures of the cooks in our kitchen teams.

However, we have learned – often through bitter experience – that you can't just present a plate of complex new flavours to children and expect them to eat it. We've taken to thinking of it as 'The Journey' and we talk a lot about it, particularly when we are starting to work with a new school. The Journey means that we recognise that some flavours and textures can be challenging and that, while they are the destination, they are not the starting point.

"The vegetables, in my opinion, are actually very nice. Last year I used to hate them, but now I really like them."
Mandeville School pupil, Mimina

We can't afford to become cocky about kids eating fresh fish or unfamiliar spices, or any food that is different or new. Every year, in every school, after the long summer break, The Journey begins again. We strip it back, start with good, plain food and then gradually introduce more complex flavours and textures. That is the nature of working with children; they keep us on our toes.

"It's more challenging than any restaurant kitchen I've worked in and the children are tougher than any restaurant critic I've ever come across!" *Nicole*

REAL FOOD

While we're on the subject, let's take a minute to talk about processed food and, in particular, ultra-processed food. This is defined as any food that has been through so many processes that it no longer resembles its original ingredients. It

often has a list of scientific-sounding ingredients that don't sound like food, including flavourings, additives and preservatives. Think packaged biscuits and cakes, salty snacks, industrial bread and sweetened breakfast cereals. At the time of writing, this kind of food accounts for over half the food bought in the UK. Yes, HALF.

It's a hard habit to break as, if you're anything like us, sneaking towards the biscuit tin at teatime is almost impossible to resist. Our bodies crave sugar and fat in order to lay down energy in case of lean times ahead and they have done so since the dawn of time. Ultra-processed food is, simply put, addictive.

At Chefs in Schools, we talk instead about real food. What we mean by 'real food' is food that is prepared from whole ingredients and doesn't contain additives, flavourings or preservatives. The gravy for our roasts comes from the roasting juices, and the custard for our puddings is made from fresh whole milk. When we take a delivery from our suppliers, the carrots may be wonky, the potatoes can have earth on them and the chicken has bones in it.

Our simple belief, backed up by research, is that, if you eat as much unprocessed food as possible, you will be living a healthier, more nourished and happier life, for your children, yourself and our planet.

Nicole and the teams have rules and aims that shape the menus and recipes they are continually developing. In some schools, the dish can change, depending on who's cooking it. In other kitchens, the recipes are set in stone after years of crafting. There is no hard and fast way of working but there are some main ideas that all of our teams keep in mind:

Fresh and seasonal: We source fresh, seasonal ingredients from incredible suppliers. Packets and powders are not used in the kitchens. This keeps nutrients high and the environmental cost low.

Colourful: We plan our menus around the whole rainbow of vegetables and fruit. The more variety in colours, the more vitamins and minerals, ensuring a nutritionally varied diet.

Varied: We use a variety of cooking methods (roasting, baking, steaming more than frying) and, where possible, a variety of ingredients within food groups (different grains, pulses, meat and fish). This ensures that we are not getting too hung up on easy (and often popular) but not very nourishing options, such as deep-frying, and in turn it stimulates biodiversity – in the land, and in our gut.

In our schools, the kitchen teams also make their own bread and yogurt, which helps to keep costs down and added ingredients out. We've included recipes for these here, too. Our Yogurt (p. 134) is mild and fresh and has a homemade-ness about it that money can't buy. Soda Bread is the first cookery lesson our Reception classes take, but don't let that put you off – it's the first recipe that students at renowned cookery school, Ballymaloe, learn too. At our schools, we make basics from scratch because it's the restaurant way, and it's good kitchen economy. At home, it's comforting to know exactly what has gone into each dish – you worry less about a bag of crisps here and there.

At the same time, we don't underestimate the size of the task that cooking from scratch is at the end of a day's work. At school, that's our job, and we have a team to do it. At home, it can seem like a never-ending mountain to climb, even for the most accomplished cook. However, it's worth remembering that, as recipes become familiar, they get quicker and easier. Many of the recipes in this collection take just a few minutes to prepare and others are good for doubling up, so you can put half in the freezer. Some are more complex, for when you feel like flexing your kitchen muscles, and some are fiddly and fun to make – ideal for smaller fingers to help out.

Whether a professional chef or a home cook, we are all on a journey in the kitchen. For many, we hope this book is a good companion to have along the way and also helps you answer that never-ending question: 'What's for dinner?'

WE EAT FIRST WITH OUR EYES

"I remember when we started to change our Friday fish dinner at Gayhurst. Oli (my sous-chef at the time, and now a chef trainer with us) and I made a plan to serve roughly puréed minted peas, and that we would quenelle them. Quenelling is a slow process – you take two spoons and shift the food from one to the other until it takes on the soft curved shape of the spoon. By the time we'd done 100 plates, I'm not sure whether we or the kids were closer to tears! We had to ditch the quenelling idea but we've never given up on making our dishes look appealing to eat. Like in a restaurant, we always keep a gastro of fresh herbs by the pass so that we can garnish each child's plate as we serve them." Nicole.

One of the great pleasures of eating in restaurants is how beautiful the food can look on the plate. Much of this is done with garnishes, such as herbs, edible flowers, tiny salad leaves, lemon peel, finely chopped raw vegetables and more – in fact, anything that adds colour and drama to a dish.

Thousands of Instagram stories make it look easy and yet, at home, most of us are not that focused on what food looks like. Often, it's enough of a juggle simply to find a dish everyone will agree on and get it on the table at more or less the right time.

In schools, one of the big shifts away from traditional school food was in our presentation. In our opinion, when the food looks and smells good, we are halfway there. A chef offers a garnish to a plate as it is served and the kids are allowed to refuse it – like all changes, accepting 'green bits' on top of your plate can take a bit of getting used to. However, over the course of a year, most will accept, and even start to enjoy, a pretty plate of food.

Many of the recipes in this book are garnished in a restaurant fashion because we want to show how attractive the food can look and give ideas for how to turn the most everyday of dishes into something special.

IT'S NOT JUST WHAT WE EAT, IT'S HOW WE EAT, TOO

"It really helps when the teachers sit with the children and chat about the food, encouraging the children to try everything on their plate." *Louise Nichols, Executive Head, Gayhurst*

If cooking food makes us human, sharing it gives us our humanity. So much more than eating happens around a table. It is where wisdom is passed on, alliances are formed and problems are solved. It is how food turns from nutrition to nourishment. Sitting down to eat together is one of the most important – if not the most important – aspects to developing a good relationship with real food.

We've found this at school, too. The chefs might make food that fills the corridors with wonderful smells, looks beautiful on the plate and tastes as good as any food in a restaurant but, unless the whole school sits down to eat it together, the power and joy of it evaporates. We aim to put food at the heart of the school day and this means getting everyone on board: the teachers in the classrooms, the midday supervisors in the dining hall, the chefs in the kitchen – and of course, the pupils. It involves working with the adults to model a 'try-something-new' attitude. When staff in a school sit down to eat with pupils, the battle is already half-won.

"When I last visited Soho Parish, the receptionist was telling me about his favourite dish – mushroom bulgogi – and how much he looks forward to eating it. They also had photos of the food and menus in reception, so school food was there to greet you when you arrived and marked out as important. To hear him talking so passionately about the food was a proud moment. Recently, some teachers started posting photos of their lunch online, as if they'd been to a restaurant. A few classes also sent handwritten thank-you cards to the chef. When we know they're talking about the food and want to sit with the children and eat it together,

that tells us that the kitchen teams are at the heart of a school." Danielle, Head of Communications

The holy grail of serving food well in school is called 'Family-Style Dining'. This is where children sit at mixed-age tables with a teacher or adult who serves the food from a platter. This is dependent on the type of dining hall a school has, and few are able to make it work. At home, though, it's yours for the making. There are many reasons why eating together makes sense. It is easier for whoever is shopping and cooking, it is cheaper, it is joyful (well, not always, but often enough). More than that is the sense of anchoring around a table that enables food to become a connection point between health, family and community that creates positive ripples through the fabric of life.

YOUR EATING ENVIRONMENT

Making a school dinner hall an attractive place to eat is extremely challenging. Usually a multi-purpose space, it has terrible acoustics and long hard tables. Even so, a few small touches can transform a meal. It is one of the main reasons why we put sharing platters of pretty salads and vegetables on the tables before the children come in. We flavour our jugs of drinking water with the sliced peel of orange, lemon or cucumber and put these out too. These small details make the table seem inviting and help build anticipation for what is to come.

TEACHING KIDS ABOUT FOOD IS HOW THEY LEARN TO EAT WELL

"I remember when Nicole brought some Japanese rice growers to assembly to explain to the children how rice is grown. Karen, the Headteacher, was told that all she had to do was introduce them to the children. The Japanese farmers and their translator started to talk in very quiet voices about rice production without any visuals. Karen could barely hear what the translator was saying herself but tried gallantly to relay it to 300 energetic children while they lost interest and were desperate to go out to play. Then, the rice farmers gave a grain of rice to each child to hold. What happened next is best forgotten and an assembly experience Karen would not like to repeat in a hurry." Louise

When Nicole started as Head Chef at Gayhurst, she decided that the best way to introduce new food was with Food Appreciation sessions in the classroom. The teachers were somewhat taken aback when she proceeded to march around the school on Friday mornings, bearing huge, dead, raw fish to show the kids before cooking them. Luckily, she had a steadfast supporter in Louise, and their food education became a journey of adventure.

Many kids don't know where food comes from. In a survey of urban primary school children, one in three believe pasta is made from meat and cheese comes from plants.

Learning about food's journey from field, farm or sea to plate is a crucial step in being able to distinguish between processed food and 'real' food. To us, it's vitally important to show kids where food comes from and what it looks like before it has been prepared and packed up – even if it's a dead animal.

"Last week we did a rabbit and crème fraîche braise. It created a real buzz and quite a lot of drama. Food can be a vehicle of social mobility so I think it's important that kids from all kinds of backgrounds get to experience really interesting innovative food. We had about 25 takers out of 200, which I was really chuffed about. Even one would have been a triumph." Jacob, Head Chef, Woodmansterne

Getting kids excited about food goes hand in hand with the food transformation in the dining halls. It's been formalised since the days of the fish being marched along the corridors but it still plays a hugely important role in the children's willingness to try new tastes. Wherever possible, we link food education directly to new food being introduced in the dining hall. For example, Julia, at Highgate Primary School, puts up drawings and

pictures of unusual ingredients where the kids line up. This decorates the hall but also helps familiarise them with new food.

At the beginning of any cookery lesson, pupils are given a chef's hat and they invent a chef name for themselves, such as 'Chef Carrot' or 'Chef Skateboard'. It's a good moment. Over the course of the seven years of primary school, we cover all the basic techniques you need to feed yourself good-value, nourishing food. These skills include: making bread and soup, preparing and chopping vegetables, making pasta, butchering a chicken and cooking fish over the fire. Our Reception class starts by making soda bread – as simple as mixing flour with buttermilk, bicarbonate of soda and salt. They take their loaves home the same afternoon with pride, and we hope they will never be daunted by the idea of making bread in the future.

HEALTH - PEOPLE AND PLANET

"When we first set out, we were quite idealistic – we wanted to do really healthy food. We poured loads of time and love into doing a big winter salad, and it just fell on its face. We started to realise that, every day that we tried to sell purely 'healthy food' we were losing customers. Now, we make interesting fresh food every day and the point is to get kids really excited about it." Jacob, Head Chef, Woodmansterne

Good health is at the heart of our mission.

It is, in fact, the very point of our existence and yet we don't talk about it all that much – not to the kids at least. We have found, through hard-learned experience, that the fastest way of turning children off new food is to label it 'healthy'. So, we work on getting them to like food that is healthy. We don't mean a diet packed with 'superfoods' but simply a variety of real food cooked from fresh ingredients, low in sugar and anything processed and lots of vegetables. We just want them to love real food; it's as simple as that.

Food education has come a long way over the past twenty years. 'Healthy eating' is a concept that all children now learn as part of the curriculum, but many kids think that savoury food is 'healthy' and sweet food is 'unhealthy'. We believe that no matter how basic your space and limited your resources, you can still engage and excite children with nature's journey from plant to plate. Even in the most urban of schools, we bring in whole foods to sniff and smell, plant herbs in planters to touch and taste and grow mushrooms in classroom cupboards. The more children become familiar with real, whole food the better chance they have of making good choices around it – and of living a healthy life.

In school, we have rolling fortnightly menus that change seasonally – it helps us to plan, for ordering and for budgeting. Each week, there are two lunches that are plant-led for the whole school, then one chicken, one fish and one red meat. This reduces the volume of meat and fish we buy and cook and the environmental impact of the food served, as well as naturally increasing the vegetables the children eat. See p. 25 for some practical ideas on menu planning.

Our own health is inextricably linked to the planet's.

We keep in mind Michael Pollen's 7-word philosophy, which has been taken up by nutritionists, farmers and environmentalists alike: 'Eat Food. Mostly Plants. Not too much.' By reducing our reliance on meat and fish, by committing to quality meat that is not intensively reared, and fish that is sustainably sourced, we are reducing our impact on the land. By cooking a broad range of ingredients, we are hoping to help encourage biodiversity, both in farming and in our gut.

Like restaurants do, we work closely with suppliers to improve packaging and we prepare as much as we can in-house, which enables chefs to create as little waste as possible.

GROWING AND FORAGING

"I was in the kitchen doing some ordering one day when one of the playground supervisors came up to share a story with me, laughing. She had seen a little girl in the corner at breaktime, chewing something. She rushed up to her and crossly asked her what it was, telling her to spit it out. A little green parcel landed on the concrete at her feet. 'It's only a bit of fennel, Miss!'" Nicole

It's easy to forget that plenty of food is free or nearly free. You can forage for some and you can grow some, even without much space. We work in primarily urban schools, where families have little access to farming and the natural food cycle. All our schools run some kind of farming project. It can be as small as a few containers for herbs in the playground, or growing mushrooms in a cupboard, but the children all get involved.

For this reason, we made the building of our own cookery school, the Hackney School of Food, our first project. It's set in a walled garden with raised beds for productive gardening. Our cookery workshops there are divided equally between working in the garden and cooking in the kitchen.

"Early on, Nicole and I used to talk about how we could give better cooking lessons for children. We wanted them to touch, feel and smell vegetables and fruit and really sense what it was. Part of that was being able to see the ingredients grow and so the Hackney School of Food was born. I love seeing everyone smile as they walk on to what used to be a derelict site and see the chefs really celebrating our produce." Louise, Executive Head, LEAP Federation

Few of us have the time or space to grow much food, but if you have room on a balcony or in the garden or even on your windowsill, planting a few seeds in pots will still be worthwhile. The kids love to get their hands dirty and help out in the garden. They enjoying digging and even weeding, and plates of vegetables are eaten up without a murmur, once Chef Tom has shown them how to prep, cook and dress them.

KITCHEN SMARTS

This section is designed to help you stock and manage your kitchen efficiently so that you have everything you need to get going. It includes storecupboard and kit lists, information about nutrition and portion sizes, plus menu planning and our 'master recipes'. These are the recipes we use most often and which will come up time and again throughout the book.

ESSENTIAL KIT

You can make almost all of these recipes with reasonably basic kit. However, the one extra piece that we turn to most often is a blender. A basic stick blender will be able to do most jobs, though a smoothie-style blender will work, too.

large sharp knife
small paring knife
bread knife
small serrated knife
wooden spoon
chopping board
mixing bowl – large
mixing bowl – small
large ovenproof casserole
medium saucepan with lid
small saucepan with lid
steamer basket
pestle and mortar
whisk
tin opener
vegetable peeler
colander
sieve
lemon zester
grater
slotted spoon
metal spatula
rubber spatula

900-g/2-lb sandwich tin
2 x 20-cm/8-inch round loose-bottomed cake tins
20 x 30-cm/8 x 12-inch baking tin
2 x roasting tins
stick blender with blender and whisk attachment
food processor – not essential but very useful

ESSENTIAL STORECUPBOARD INGREDIENTS

These basic ingredients make up our storecupboard. There are notes with * below on our more unusual favourites that we turn to in order to add texture, depth and extra flavour.

Grains and pulses
cannellini beans
chickpeas
chopped tomatoes
dried red lentils
frozen peas
noodles
oats
pasta – 1 short (e.g. penne) and 1 long
(e.g. spaghetti)
rice: brown basmati, white basmati, risotto
sweetcorn
tinned lentils

Oils and vinegars
apple cider vinegar
balsamic vinegar
coconut oil*
extra virgin olive oil
olive oil

Essentials, condiments, pickles
capers
coconut milk
gherkins
harissa*
honey
low-salt vegetable stock cube
mayo
panko breadcrumbs*
preserved lemon*
soy sauce
tahini*
white miso paste*

Baking
baking powder
bicarbonate of soda
golden caster sugar
plain flour
spelt flour
vanilla extract
white bread flour
wholemeal flour
yeast

Essential dried herbs and spices
black pepper
chilli flakes
coriander seeds and ground coriander
cumin seeds and ground cumin
dried mint
turmeric
sea salt
star anise
sweet smoked paprika

A FEW OF OUR FAVOURITE THINGS

We return time and again to a few special ingredients that can always be relied on to build in depths of flavour and texture. When it comes to basic seasoning, we prefer sea salt, and for pepper, freshly ground black pepper unless specified otherwise:

Fresh herbs – rosemary, parsley, basil, coriander: We can't extol the virtues of fresh herbs enough as, by adding real freshness and zing, they are the fastest and easiest way to make food look and taste more vibrant. Food shops and markets often sell huge bunches of herbs at a much cheaper price than supermarkets. Growing your own in a pot on the windowsill also makes an easy and rewarding project to share with the family.

Harissa: This fiery North African pepper and chilli paste adds a real bang. We love to use the more mellow, fragrant rose harissa, which is made by Belazu.

Miso paste: Miso paste, the fermented soybean paste that Japanese miso soup is made from, adds a mellow savouriness to all sorts of dishes, as well as a variety of micronutrients. We use white miso paste, which is the mildest and sweetest.

Panko breadcrumbs: These very light Japanese breadcrumbs make for an extra crispy coating. Because they are dry, they keep for months in a sealed container. However, if you have none to hand, simply whizz any leftover bread into breadcrumbs, using a food processor.

Preserved lemon: Lemons preserved in salt are a staple of the Middle Eastern pantry. They add a tangy depth to dishes.

Tahini: This creamy paste of ground sesame seeds is a Middle Eastern staple. The hidden glue that holds together hummus, it's also a wonderful marinade and dressing and even tastes great sweetened (if you try our Tahini Brownies on p. 151 and Apple and Tahini Buns on p. 137, you'll see).

NUTRITION

If the colours we wave are all about the joy and pleasure of real food, the flagpole they are mounted on is good nutrition. We are committed partners in the Biteback 2030 campaign to cut childhood obesity by half by 2030, and we sit on the panel that evaluates school food standards. A hot lunch for some children at many of the schools we work with will be the only meal they eat in a day. The balance of nutrients must be right.

To do that, we subscribe to the School Food Charter's nutritional values and we use the guides provided by them to calculate a careful balance of nourishing food. You can find them at http://www.schoolfoodplan.com/actions/school-food-standards/. For cooking at home, we have translated these into hand sizes, to make them easier to follow.

FOOD PORTIONS

The best guide to portions is to use the hand size of whoever is eating that plate. It's impossible to be completely accurate – every day differs, depending on how active it has been – and particularly, for children, whether they are going through a growth spurt. However, it's a good indication.

Vegetables (non-starchy, such as beans, broccoli, peas)
Two hands cupped together is the minimum amount for each meal. Include more if you can, with as many different colours as possible, as these indicate and add a different range of vitamins and minerals.

Starchy vegetables and vegetable protein, such as pulses
These foods include potatoes, rice, pasta, bread, couscous and batter. Pulses are chickpeas, lentils and dried or tinned beans. The volume of these two groups of food should be the size of a closed fist.

Fish
A flat hand indicates the right volume of fish.

Meat
The palm of a hand and about the same thickness, is a good guide for meat. Cured and salted meat, such as bacon and salami, should be eaten in moderation.

If you want to reduce the amount of animal protein in your diet, replace with a vegetable protein equivalent. See p. 23 for the vegetarian protein chart.

Snacks – vegetables, fruit and nuts
A handful of vegetables, fruit and nuts counts as a single portion (one of your 'five-a-day') and makes a good size for snacks.

Where possible, we use organic ingredients. Our budgets at school are extremely tight – we have found the most impact for the least difference in cost is in eggs and milk. Where we can't use organic, we check the changing lists at the Pesticide Action Network, which grades food into the most pesticide-heavy, enabling you to choose where buying organic would have most impact. See https://www.pan-uk.org/dirty-dozen/

A NOTE ABOUT PROTEIN

These days, whether out of personal belief, animal welfare or environmental awareness, we are all eating more vegetable protein. This changes the 'meat and two veg' style of eating that was historically prevalent in the UK to something that looks a bit different on the plate. This means recognising that protein can come in many forms, whether it's the yogurt dip in the middle of the table, to a seed crunch that garnishes a roast cauliflower. The British Nutrition Foundation recommends, on average, 19.7g of protein a day for children aged 4–6, and 28.3g of protein for those aged 7–10. Comprehensive details for nutritional requirements for the whole family can be found at nutrition.org.uk.

An example of how vegetable protein can work across the day for a 7–10-year-old who requires approximately 28g of protein a day is:
Breakfast = 1 tablespoon of peanut butter (4.2g)
1 x cup soya milk (8.9g)
Lunch = 2 x slices wholemeal bread (8.8g)
Dinner = 2 handfuls of lentils or chickpeas (7.8g)
= 29g protein

It is worth noting that some essential vitamins, in particular B12, are harder to capture from an entirely plant-based diet and supplements may be required. It is advised to consult your doctor or health care practitioner before switching your family to an entirely vegan diet.

VEGETARIAN PROTEIN CHART

This chart outlines vegetarian proteins. Whether vegetarian or not, including more vegetable protein allows you to reduce your consumption of meat and fish, which in turn reduces your costs and your impact on the environment.

FOOD	PORTION	PROTEIN (g) (approximate)
Cottage cheese	175g / 6oz	13
Hemp seeds	30g / 4 tablespoons	13
Firm tofu	100g / 3½oz	12.5
Pulses (e.g. dried or canned beans, split peas or lentils), cooked	100g / 3¼oz (2 cupped hands)	12
Egg, chicken	120g / 2 large	12
Cheese	50g / 1¾oz (½ palm of hand)	12
Peanuts	40g / 4 tablespoons	9
Peanut butter	30g / 2 tablespoons	8
Almonds	40g / 4 tablespoons	8
Almond butter	30g / 2 tablespoons	7
Yogurt	175g / 6oz	7
Sunflower or pumpkin seeds	30g / 4 tablespoons	6
Walnuts	40g / 4 tablespoons	5
Cashews	40g / 4 tablespoons	5
Cow's milk	125ml / 4fl oz	4.5
Whomeal bread	35g / 1 slice	4
Dried pasta, cooked	100g / 3¼oz	4
Quinoa, cooked	90g / 3¼oz	4
Nut milk	125ml / 4fl oz	4
Soya milk	125ml / 4fl oz	3.5
Rice, cooked	100g / 3¼oz	2.5
Oat milk	125ml / 4fl oz	2

SIMPLE SWAPS

It's easy to get stuck in a rut with shopping and cooking habits. We've put together some ideas to help you shake up your thinking, whether it's shaving your budget or packing in some extra nutrition.

Replace
– white bread with wholegrain or spelt
– white pasta with 50/50
– white rice with a combination of white and brown
– white rice or couscous with quinoa
– white sugar with unrefined sugars (e.g. golden caster, muscovado), maple syrup or honey
– plain flour with white spelt flour

BUDGETING

Sticking to a budget is at the heart of any school kitchen success. Here, the chefs we work with share some golden rules from their kitchens.

1. Reduce the quantity of expensive food, rather than compromise on the quality of the ingredients

"For fish Friday, we sometimes make fresh fish-finger sandwiches – the fish is top quality, provided by Brixham Seafish, but we only need a very small amount for each portion." Jake, Totteridge Academy

2. Cook seasonally

"Natoora has made us a seasonal produce calendar so that we can ensure we are always cooking seasonally. Last week, I worked out with a chef that, in the winter, a whole box of apples is the same price as a single punnet of strawberries." Nerissa, Chef Trainer

3. Eat less meat

"The whole school eats vegetarian twice a week, not just as an option. Instead of calling it 'Vegetarian Lasagne' or 'Vegetable Pizza', we just use the names Lasagne and Pizza. Sometimes it's simply a question of language that enables a shift." Charlie, Stormont House

4. Swap to cheaper cuts

"Coming from a family who owned restaurants in Malta, I was given bone marrow from a very young age and, even though I ate it without question, I was always intrigued by it. I think it was this that triggered my interest in cooking meat on the bone and using the most flavoursome cuts of meat. If you take meat with a significant amount of muscle – such as rump, cheeks, neck and oxtail – and braise it for a long period of time, this dissolves the collagen and both gives you an intense flavour and results in the softest piece of meat, which you can then eat in different ways over the week." Nicole

5. Balance your budget across the week

"We keep our vegetarian days really cheap, with meals such as tomato pasta (p. 31) or dhal (p. 62) with rice. These then offset the cost of our more expensive meals, such as the hake on p. 51." Helen, Head Chef, Gayhurst

6. Calculate your volumes carefully, and use up leftovers

"We've gone down to close to zero food waste in the kitchen by working with chefs to change the way they think – now, we cook the whole broccoli, including the stalk, and roast cauliflower with the leaves on. Instead of discarding the seeds and strands from the core of the pumpkin, we dry them out overnight then grind them to make tahini. It's about opening your mind and asking yourself the question, 'What can I do with this that's going to feed the kids safely?'" Nicole.

7. Make your own basics when you can

"When I arrived at Gayhurst as the new Head Chef, one of the first things I did was to train SouSou, one of the existing kitchen team, to bake bread. It saved us an astonishing £90 a day, as well as avoiding the hidden sugar and preservatives that come in many shop-bought loaves. We offer bread at lunchtime, and at breakfast clubs and after-school clubs, and then use breadcrumb leftovers in some of our other dishes." Nicole

GOOD HABITS FOR SAVING MONEY

"When I arrived at Gayhurst, I knew I needed to slash the budget at the same time as improving the quality of ingredients. To achieve this, I took the whole school vegetarian two days a week. This enabled me to radically cut costs on some meals, which meant I had more to spend on others. The final part in the puzzle was to get some great suppliers on board. With the help of Brixham Seafish and Devon Rose Meats, we were able to order the same quality ingredients that were served in top London restaurants. Brixham still supports many of our schools with fish, as close to cost price as they can. They are one of the great unsung heroes of our school food."
Nicole

– Where possible, buy from experts: markets, grocers, fishmongers and butchers. They will always have advice for getting more value from your shopping and can point you in the right direction so you can benefit from seasonal gluts or discounts.
– Buy in bulk: double your volumes and freeze half.
– Choose seasonal fruit and veg over year-round produce.
– Choose wonky or unprepared veg over perfect vegetables, which carry a premium price tag.
– Swap out canned pulses for dried: they can be cooked up in batches and frozen in portions.

MENU PLANNING

Thoughtful planning is the key to balancing both budget and nutrition in our schools. The Head Chefs run a rolling two-week menu with seasonal variations, which allows them to work closely with suppliers to ensure they are getting the best deal possible. At home, allowing a bit more flexibility enables you to experiment with flavours, and use up leftovers.

It's a good idea to pin up a meal plan at home, somewhere everyone can see it, such as the fridge, and start by filling in a few suggestions. Leave space for the rest of the family to have some input as of course children like the chance to have their say, and this often results in them being more willing to try something new.

GET AHEAD ONCE A WEEK TO SAVE TIME ON THE NIGHT

– Put aside some time each week when you can prep ahead and cook up some of the basics. This will mean you can then get food on the table fast when you need it most.
– Chop and fry double the volume of onions and freeze half.
– Blitz a whole head of garlic in oil and freeze in small portions, such as in ice-cube trays.
– Batch-cook basic sauces, e.g. Tomato and Miso on p. 31 or Dhal on p. 62.
– Grate more cheese than you need for pasta and freeze in portions.

MASTER RECIPES

These are the recipes we return to time and again. Here you'll find 'how-tos' for everyday staples such as rice and pasta, as well as our knockout tomato sauce (p. 31) – as good tossed through a basic bowl of spaghetti as it is with an elegant plate of baked hake (p. 51). Here too, are some sauces and sides you can make in volume to pep up the simplest of offerings – our chilli sauce will transform an omelette as well as the gyozas on p. 88; while a spoon or two of salsa verde (p. 30) will make a plain chicken drumstick or piece of fish (such as the mackerel on p. 46) instantly more exciting.

HOW TO COOK RICE

Our go-to rice is basmati, both brown or white. In fact, we often combine both, which allows us to tuck in some extra fibre. In order to do this, you will need to cook them separately and fold them together when you fluff them up. Lots of people are scared of cooking rice, but once you understand this basic method, you can apply it to lots of different types of rice; you may just need to adjust the cooking times slightly. If you cook too much rice, you can keep it in the fridge for a couple of days, or freeze it on the day of cooking and defrost it in the fridge. Either way, cool it down as quickly as possible after cooking, and make sure it's piping hot when you reheat it. Frozen and defrosted rice is perfect for making fried rice (p. 63)

HOW TO COOK WHITE BASMATI RICE

FEEDS 4

300g/10½oz basmati rice
400ml/14fl oz water

First, place the rice in a pan with a tight-fitting lid (you'll need this later) and cover with a generous amount of water. Swirl it around with your hand or a spoon for a minute to release the starch and allow it to soak for 15 minutes.

Drain the rice through a sieve and rinse under cold running water for a couple of minutes to remove the starch. Now, return the rice to the pot with the measured water. Bring to a simmer and cook with the lid on for 10 minutes. Then, switch off the heat, wrap the lid in a tea towel and replace back on the pot to absorb excess steam.

Give the pan one more 30-second blast of heat to create as much steam as possible and then switch off the heat and allow the pot to steam for 5 minutes. The rice can then sit for up to 20 minutes before eating. Remove the lid and fluff up with a fork to serve.

HOW TO COOK BROWN BASMATI RICE

This is the same method as white basmati, but with adjusted cooking times. Ideally, it's worth soaking brown rice for longer to reduce the cooking time.

FEEDS 4

400g/14oz brown basmati rice
480ml/16½fl oz water

First, place the rice in a pan with a tight-fitting lid (you'll need this later) and add a generous amount of water. Swirl it around with your hand or a spoon for a minute to release the starch then pour out the water and repeat. Fill with water and allow to soak for 45 minutes, then drain, rinsing under running water. Return to the pot with the measured water. Bring to a simmer and cook with the lid on for 25 minutes. Then, switch off the heat, wrap the lid in a tea towel and allow the pot to steam for 15 minutes. The rice can then sit for up to 30 minutes before eating. Remove the lid and fluff up with a fork to serve.

HOW TO COOK PASTA

Our preferred pasta is 50:50 white and wholemeal (Napolina make a good version), which gives you the best of both in terms of taste, texture and nutritional value, but you can use your pasta of choice in any of our recipes. You will want about 100g/3½oz cooked pasta per person, and 125g/4½oz for teenagers.

Bring a large pan of water with a tablespoon of sea salt to the boil. Add your pasta and return it to the boil. Check the packet for cooking time; it can vary but is usually around 10 minutes. To make it al dente (our preference), cook for 1 minute less than the recommended time. To use in a pasta bake, cook for 2 minutes less. Drain, reserving a tablespoon of the cooking water to loosen any sauce. Toss thoroughly with your sauce and divide between plates to serve.

HOW TO COOK QUINOA

Quinoa makes a great alternative to rice, high in protein with a lovely nutty flavour.

FEEDS 4

200g/7oz quinoa
500ml/18fl oz water

Rinse the quinoa in a sieve under cold running water for 2 minutes to remove any bitterness, then place, along with the measured water, in a pot with a tight-fitting lid. Bring to a simmer and cook with the lid on for 10 minutes. Then, switch off the heat, wrap the lid in a tea towel and replace back on the pot to absorb excess steam. Give the pan one more 30-second blast of heat to create as much steam as possible and then switch off the heat and allow to steam for 5 minutes. The quinoa can then sit for up to 20 minutes before eating. Remove the lid and fluff up with a fork to serve.

HOW TO MAKE MEDIUM EGG NOODLES

1 nest of noodles per person

Place plenty of water (3:1 water to noodle ratio) in a large pan and bring to the boil. When boiling, drop in the noodles and boil for 3 minutes. Fill a large bowl with cold water. When the noodles are cooked, drain through a sieve and drop into the cold water.

Once cool, drain thoroughly. They can sit until you are ready to use them for a couple of hours, or refrigerate for 24 hours. Reheat with a little oil or in your sauce of choice.

HOW TO MAKE COUSCOUS

Most kids love the unchallenging texture and mildness of couscous. You can stir through chopped cooked veg or almost any leftovers and toss with salad dressing to make it into a quick meal.

FEEDS 4

240g/8oz couscous
1 tablespoon extra virgin olive oil
½ teaspoon salt

Place the couscous, olive oil and salt in a heatproof bowl and stir to mix. Pour over 240ml/8fl oz boiling water, immediately cover with a clean tea towel and put to one side to steam.

After 10 minutes, remove the tea towel and fluff up the couscous with a fork. Cooked couscous will keep in the fridge for up to 3 days.

HOW TO ROAST BUTTERNUT SQUASH (AND OTHER VEGETABLES)

You can add herbs and garlic to the tray for extra flavour. Chopped rosemary and a few garlic cloves are delicious.

1 butternut squash, peeled, deseeded and
   roughly chopped
3 tablespoons olive oil
½ teaspoon sea salt

Preheat the oven to 220°C fan/240°C/475°F/gas mark 9.

Tip the butternut squash into a roasting tin and toss with the olive oil until nicely coated. Sprinkle with salt and any other flavourings and mix again.

Roast for 25–35 minutes (if you are cooking very dense roots such as beetroot and celeriac you will need longer), until the vegetables are just tender and beginning to burnish.

HOW TO COOK CHICKPEAS IN BULK

There is nothing wrong with canned chickpeas (great pantry staple). But if you have time, cooking your own from dried is cheaper and nicer and they freeze really well.

MAKES 1KG/2LB 4OZ CHICKPEAS, EQUIVALENT TO 4 X 400G/14OZ CANS

500g/1lb 2oz dried chickpeas

Pour the chickpeas into a large saucepan, cover generously with cold water and leave to soak overnight.

In the morning, drain the chickpeas, then put them back in the same saucepan, cover with cold water and bring to the boil over a medium-high heat. Skim any scum off the top and then turn the heat down to a simmer. Cook until very soft – 30 to 60 minutes, depending on the size and age of your chickpeas.

Drain very well, reserving the cooking liquid (aquafaba) if you'd like to use it. Pour the chickpeas into a couple of large freezer bags, lying them as flat as possible. Next time you need cooked chickpeas for a recipe, use directly from the freezer. (1 x 400g/14oz can cooked chickpeas before draining = 250g/9oz cooked chickpeas.)

CHILLI SAUCE

We recommend you make this in bulk – it is fab! Hot and a bit sour with a tiny hint of sweetness, it makes everything more exciting. Eat it alongside so many different dishes throughout the week, like Special Fried Rice on p. 63 and Prawn Toast on p. 60.

MAKES 1 JAM JAR

3 tablespoons sesame oil
6 garlic cloves, chopped
5-cm/ 2-inch piece of fresh ginger, peeled and finely grated
2–4 large red chillies, deseeded and finely diced
3 tablespoons honey
120ml/4fl oz rice vinegar
Pinch of sea salt

Place everything in a blender and blend until smooth. Pour the sauce into a pan and simmer on a very low heat for 2 hours. Allow to cool, then transfer to an airtight container and keep in the fridge for a month.

CHEF'S NOTES

Some kids will find this really hot! Stir through a tablespoon of yogurt to temper the heat.

BASIC STOCK

Miso is a great source of umami, which is the fifth taste element (the other four are salty, sweet, bitter and sour). It doesn't have an English word to describe it, so we think of it as lip-smacking savouriness. We use it in combination with vegetable stock cubes to add depth and flavour.

MAKES 500ML/18FL OZ

1 vegetable stock cube
1 tablespoon white miso paste

Place the ingredients in a heatproof bowl or jug, pour over 500ml/18fl oz boiling water and stir to dissolve. Use wherever stock is required.

SALSA VERDE

This recipe is from Nicole's book, *Salt, Butter, Bones*. The lovage can be substituted by celery leaves or indeed any summer herb, such as basil or mint, but if you do come across lovage, the strong flavour is very intriguing for kids. It makes them crunch up their little faces when trying it for the first time but they often like the bitterness.

ENOUGH FOR 1 X 500ML/18FL OZ JAR OR 2 X JAM JARS

50g/1¾oz picked and finely chopped lovage (or celery leaves)
50g/1¾oz picked flat-leaf parsley leaves and tender stems, coarsely chopped (about ½ large bunch)
50g/1¾oz picked coriander leaves and tender stems, coarsely chopped (about ½ large bunch)
50g/1¾oz chives, coarsely chopped
3 large garlic cloves, grated or crushed
2 teaspoons baby capers
2 anchovies from a tin, drained and roughly chopped
2 tablespoons red wine vinegar
100ml/3½fl oz olive oil, plus extra to cover
Freshly ground black pepper

Blitz or pulse all the ingredients until you have a textured paste. Store in an airtight container in the fridge, covered in a slick of oil. It will keep for a week or so.

CHEF'S NOTES

This is a great 'home' for any herbs that are slightly bruised. If you can't get any of the particular herbs listed, replace with extra parsley.

TOMATO AND MISO SAUCE

When Nicole started working in one school, she discovered that iron was being added to food to meet nutritional requirements... in the form of chocolate powder. Wanting to lose the junk but preserve the iron, she began to use miso paste, which added a savoury depth to dishes as well as packing a nutritional punch. This is our go-to recipe; we turn to it all the time and it's our back-up option for every school lunch. If a child is struggling, they can always come back for a plate of pasta tossed in this sauce. You can also stir it through a plain risotto, bake fish on top of it (see our recipe for hake on p. 51), or toss meatballs in it (p. 70). You name it, it's always there for you.

MAKES 3 BATCHES, ENOUGH TO FEED 4 PEOPLE EACH

2 tablespoons olive oil

1 red onion, peeled and roughly chopped

1 garlic clove, peeled and finely chopped

1 teaspoon ground cumin

2-cm/1-inch piece of fresh ginger, peeled and grated

1 tablespoon balsamic vinegar

3 x 400g/14oz cans plum tomatoes

2 tablespoons miso paste

1 teaspoon salt

In a medium-size saucepan (for which you have a lid), heat the oil over a medium heat. When hot, add the onion, garlic, cumin and ginger and cook until the onion is translucent, around 10 minutes.

Add the balsamic vinegar and scrape the bottom of the pan to get any sticky bits off.

Tip in the tomatoes, miso paste and salt and simmer, partially covered, for 30 minutes.

Allow to cool and then, using a stick blender, blitz to a smooth sauce. It will keep for 5 days in the fridge, and freezes well.

CHEF'S NOTES

If cumin is new to your kids and they're wary of strong flavours, start the journey by introducing it gradually – add an extra pinch each time you make it, until you get to 1 teaspoon. Blitz any of your leftover vegetables into this sauce, but bear in mind it will lose it's bright red colour.

OUR RECIPES

Welcome to our collection of recipes inspired by Nicole and the chefs we work with. They include a huge array of influences and ingredients from food at school and at home, here and around the world. Some are comforting, others, challenging, and together they form a snapshot of the food in the schools we work with, and a vision of how we believe children should eat – with excitement, adventure, joy. Whilst many of the flavours are complex, we believe that all of them are within reach of the home cook. That's not to promise that there's no work involved in encouraging children to try all of these foods – that's certainly a huge part of our mission. Neither can we promise that every dish will appeal to every child – it goes without saying that we all have different tastes and different moods at all different times. But all of these recipes have been thoroughly trialled and tested on the toughest customers of all – the kids we work with. And, though we say so ourselves, they are delicious!

A thought about building your menus: At school, it's the job of the chefs to cook lunch and so they are able to produce a variety of dishes for a single meal. However, we recognise that this is rarely possible in the home. For this reason, we have tried hard to incorporate multiple food groups into a main dish wherever possible, in order to reduce the number of dishes you need to cook on the side. We have also made recommendations for what would work as a side dish to complement the meal. Once you become familiar with the dishes, you may like to combine them into a single meal – for example, the Baked Hake with Tomato Sauce (p. 51) is shown with the Maltese Potatoes (p. 114). But, for a quicker, simpler version, it's also great with rice or a baked potato.

SYMBOLS

We have developed a series of symbols to help you figure out what sort of recipe each one is; the kind of situation it will work in, how long it will take and whether it can be prepared in advance, etc. These are:

 'GOOD FOR THE FREEZER'
These recipes freeze well so it's a good idea to double the quantities and put a meal in the freezer for future use.

 'MAKE TOGETHER'
Get the children in the kitchen, as these are recipes they will enjoy. They involve a tactile style of cooking that is fun for all ages and the fiddly bits are still simple but ideal for little hands and fingers.

 'UNDER £1'
You'll find this on all main dishes that cost less that £1 per portion to make.

The chef's notes include suggestions for garnishes and any other chef tricks for enhancing a dish in flavour or nutrients, as well as tips for introducing more adventurous flavours to children.

A NOTE ABOUT ALLERGIES

Allergies are so prevalent these days and we are extremely respectful of that fact. At our schools, we have developed a system that identifies children who have gluten and dairy allergies, and all the schools we work with are completely nut-free, in order to protect children whose nut allergies are a real and present danger to them at all times. However, we do not particularly advocate a nut-free diet if it is safe for you and your family to eat them. Nuts are a wonderful and hugely important part of our diet, contributing good oils for our skin and bones and providing crucial micronutrients for healthy development and growth. A handful of nuts is one of the best snacks you can provide in-between meals. Therefore, our recipes do include nuts but, where they arise, we always offer a nut-free alternative.

Where milk is required in a recipe, the assumption is that it will be full-fat cow's milk, but other milks can be substituted. Where flour is referenced, unless otherwise mentioned, it is assumed to be wheat flour, though gluten-free flour can be substituted in all places apart from breadmaking.

THE
C

"Today was our pasta day. We did ox cheek ragu, braised for five hours until it was like butter. Super-dry and crispy orange peel, which had been drying overnight, went in, along with star anise and rosemary from the garden – they love that one. They really go for moules frites, too – there's nothing better than seeing a Year-7 kid walk off with a bowl of mussels. Later this week I'll do ox tongue and mustard sandwiches with pickled fennel." JACOB, HEAD CHEF, WOODMANSTERNE

NEW CLASSICS

If there is a chapter that sums up what we love about food – this is it. Joyful, clever and exciting, these recipes are particularly close to our hearts. Here you'll find new takes on familiar favourites, as well as dishes that make us smile – both to cook and to eat. The turmeric in our fish finger crumb gives them a deep golden crust, and our Bolognese (a really good one) balances out traditional mince with lentils, giving it an update that still ssings with flavour and delivers heft. Our macaroni cheese is silky and spinach-green, yet it eats just like a mac 'n' cheese should: comforting, unctuous and deeply cheesy. And our mackerel is cooked over a fire – it's how Nicole has taught the kids to cook it since her first cookery lesson at Gayhurst, back in 2013.

BOLOGNESE OUR WAY

Here, we've replaced some of the mince with lentils to reduce the cost, both financial and environmental. If you don't want to make a big batch, just halve the ingredients.

FEEDS 12

3 tablespoons olive oil

2 onions, peeled and sliced

2 leeks, finely sliced

2-cm/1-inch piece of fresh ginger, peeled and finely chopped

2 garlic cloves, peeled and finely chopped

1kg/2lb 4oz beef mince

1 x 400g/14oz can green lentils, drained

3 carrots, grated

2 courgettes, grated

2 x 400g/14oz cans chopped tomatoes

2 tablespoons tomato purée

1½ teaspoons sea salt

TO SERVE

100g/3½oz cooked spaghetti per person

50g/1¾oz grated cheese (optional)

Small bunch of basil, leaves picked

Small bunch of tarragon, leaves picked

Heat the oil in a large (flameproof) casserole (or heavy-based saucepan) for which you have a lid, and fry the onion, leek, ginger and garlic until very soft, around 15 minutes.

Scoop the cooked onion mixture out onto a plate and turn up the heat. Add the minced beef and cook until the meat has browned, then add the cooked onions back into the pan, and turn down the heat again.

In a large jug, tip in the drained lentils, grated carrot and courgette and, using a stick blender, blitz to a smooth paste. Tip this into the meat, along with the canned tomatoes, tomato purée and salt. Cover and cook over a low heat for 1 hour.

Meanwhile, cook the pasta in boiling salted water for 8–9 minutes, then drain the pasta and combine with the sauce.

Serve with grated cheese, if you like, and a garnish of chopped basil and tarragon.

CHEF'S NOTES

Bolognese can be eaten with sweet potatoes for a fast dinner, and also with rice.

TURMERIC FISH FINGERS

with Tartare

A great recipe to make with kids. The turmeric adds a golden colour to the crumb and the oats provide an unusual, knobbly texture. They are quite delicate to work with so take your time.

FEEDS 4 (MAKES 8)

Drizzle of olive oil
100g/3½oz plain flour
2 free-range eggs
75g/2¾oz panko breadcrumbs
½ teaspoon Chinese five spice
5 heaped tablespoons oats
1 teaspoon ground turmeric
500g/1lb 2oz pollock (or similar), cut into 10cm x 2cm (4in x 1in) pieces
1 lime or lemon, cut into wedges, to serve
Sea salt and black pepper

FOR THE TARTARE SAUCE
170g/5¾oz mayonnaise
30g/1oz green pitted olives, finely chopped
25g/1oz capers, finely chopped
60g/2¼oz gherkins, finely chopped
Small bunch of dill, roughly chopped
Small bunch of chervil or parsley, roughly chopped
1 teaspoon lemon juice

Preheat the oven to 220°C fan/240°C/475°F/gas mark 9 and line a large oven tray with a baking mat, drizzled with a little olive oil.

Prepare the dipping stations. Line up three lipped plates: In the first, place the flour with a big pinch of salt and pepper and mix to combine. In the second plate, crack the eggs and whisk lightly with a fork. In the third plate, add the panko, five spice, oats, turmeric and ¼ teaspoon of salt, and stir to combine.

Find a partner and assign duties – one person covers the fish in flour, then dips it in the egg, whilst the other person rolls the fish fingers in the breadcrumb mix and then places them on the lined baking tray.

Drizzle the fish fingers with a little more oil and bake for 15 minutes until golden brown and the fish is opaque.

To make the tartare, simply stir all the ingredients together. Serve the fish fingers with the tartare and a wedge of lime or lemon.

CHEF'S NOTES

If you like bold flavours, up the Chinese five spice to ¾ teaspoon.

YuTaM's PuTATu CaKES

"Like many boys his age, our youngest son, Flynn (who is 4), would present a wish list of items for supper that were exclusively carb-y and wholly white. 'Doughboy', as we like to call him, would ask for naked bread to start, followed by 'pasta with nothing', then plain potatoes and, to finish, a slice of cake. Therefore, I decided to compromise with this version of maaqouda*, which are traditional North African fried patties. It was generally very well received and became a blueprint for future meals, where I folded in different ingredients I wanted to use up. (Spinach worked well, as did roasted pepper and corn.) Flynn, however, wasn't totally impressed. 'Too many peas,' he exclaimed. He did insist, though, on having the leftovers stuffed into a sandwich that evening, with some ketchup, which kind of worked."* Yotam Ottolenghi, Patron of Chefs in Schools

FEEDS 4-6

4 large floury potatoes (about 900g/2lb) such as Maris Piper, scrubbed clean

110ml/3¾fl oz olive oil

12 spring onions, trimmed and thinly sliced

4 garlic cloves, thinly sliced

150g/5½oz frozen peas, thawed

2 teaspoons chopped fresh thyme leaves, plus a few extra sprigs to garnish

120ml/4fl oz double cream

2 large free-range eggs plus 1 yolk, beaten

60g/2¼oz Parmesan, finely grated

2 tablespoons finely chopped preserved lemon or 1 tablespoon fresh lemon zest

¾ teaspoon ground turmeric

100g/3½oz mature Cheddar, roughly grated

150g/5½oz feta, roughly crumbled

Sea salt and black pepper

Add the potatoes to a large pot and top with enough water to cover by about 4cm/1½ inches. Bring to a boil, then lower the heat to medium, cover with a lid and cook until easily pierced with a knife, about 30 minutes. Drain well. Once cool enough to handle, peel the potatoes (saving the skins for another use), and transfer them to a large bowl.

Meanwhile, add half the olive oil to a large (28-cm/11-inch) ovenproof frying pan that is at least 8cm/3 inches deep. Heat over a medium heat and, once hot, add the spring onions and garlic and cook, stirring occasionally, until soft and lightly coloured, about 6 minutes. Add the peas, thyme, ¼ teaspoon salt and plenty of pepper, then stir to combine and set aside.

Preheat the oven to 210°C fan/230°C/450°F/gas mark 8.

Add the cream, beaten eggs, Parmesan, preserved lemon, turmeric, half the Cheddar and ½ teaspoon salt to the potatoes in the large bowl. Use a potato masher to break everything down to a rough mash that is still a bit lumpy. Add the feta and the spring onion mixture and fold everything together.

Wipe the spring onion pan clean, add the remaining olive oil, then transfer it to the oven for about 5 minutes to heat up. Remove from the oven and carefully add the potato mix. Level the top, sprinkle with the remaining Cheddar and a few sprigs of thyme, if using, in the centre and return to the oven.

Reduce the oven temperature to 180°C fan/200°C/400°F/gas mark 6 and bake the cake until golden and bubbling, 25–30 minutes. Remove from the oven and set aside for 15 minutes to firm up before serving. Sprinkle with the last few thyme leaves, and serve warm, spooned directly from the pan.

JAMES'S TAHINI CHICKEN THIGHS *with Coriander Rice and Salad*

"The lemon in the marinade gives the recipe a nice bit of sharpness and the depth of flavour comes from the garlic, shallots and rosemary. Served with some brown rice and a simple fresh salad, this is a really tasty and nutritious meal, without too much hard work." James Taylor, Exec School Chef, Harrington Hill and Grasmere Schools

FEEDS 4

8 chicken thighs
1 tablespoon extra virgin olive oil
½ teaspoon sea salt

FOR THE MARINADE
100g/3½oz tahini
Juice of 1 lemon
3 garlic cloves, finely chopped
1 small shallot, very finely chopped
2 tablespoons olive oil
1 teaspoon rosemary leaves, chopped
Sea salt and black pepper

FOR THE SALAD
250g/9oz cherry tomatoes, quartered
1 cucumber, finely chopped
1 little gem lettuce, finely sliced
2 spring onions, finely sliced
2 tablespoons extra virgin olive oil
1 lime, juiced to get 1 tablespoon
Bunch of flat-leaf parsley, finely chopped

TO SERVE
1 volume of brown rice, p. 27
2 tablespoons fresh coriander, roughly chopped

You need to allow time for the chicken to marinate so start this recipe one day ahead.

First make the marinade: In a small bowl, mix the tahini with 3 tablespoons water. It will split at first but keep stirring and it will come together. Add the lemon juice, garlic, shallot, oil, rosemary and 1 teaspoon each of salt and pepper, and mix well.

Place the chicken thighs in an ovenproof dish, pour over the marinade and use your hands to thoroughly coat the chicken in the sauce. Cover with clingfilm or a large, inverted plate and keep in the fridge overnight.

The next day, preheat the oven to 190°C fan/210°C/410°F/gas mark 6½ and take the chicken out of the fridge.

For the salad, put all the ingredients in a bowl, mix gently and set aside.

Take the clingfilm off the chicken and bake in the hot oven for 45 minutes, until the skin is crispy and the chicken is cooked through.

To make the rice, follow the instructions on p. 27. When ready to eat, fluff the rice with a fork and stir through the chopped coriander leaves.

To serve, divide the rice between four bowls. Top with two chicken thighs each, drizzled with tahini sauce, and finish with a plate of salad on the side.

GREEN MAC 'N' CHEESE

Our Trustee, Thomasina Miers, was ruminating the other day on how much she'd hated cauliflower cheese when she was little. Now, loving cauliflower, and loving cheese, she wonders why. Inspired, we set about creating the ultimate, veg-packed cheesy dinner in the form of this recipe. The sauce works brilliantly with cauliflower, too (see note below), so this one's for you, Tommi!

FEEDS 4

75g/2½oz unsalted butter
5 tablespoons plain flour
1½ teaspoons English mustard powder
775ml/27¼fl oz full-fat milk
175g/6oz extra-mature Cheddar cheese, grated
1 teaspoon sweet smoked paprika
Several good gratings of nutmeg
300g/10½oz frozen spinach, defrosted and liquid squeezed out
400g/14oz small pasta, like macaroni
5 tablespoons stale breadcrumbs
40g/1½oz Parmesan cheese, grated
Sea salt and black pepper

Preheat the oven to 200°C fan/220°C/425°F/gas mark 7.

Fill a large pan with water, add a tablespoon of salt and bring to the boil – you're going to cook the pasta in this shortly.

In a medium pan, melt the butter, stir in the flour and mustard powder and season with salt and pepper. Stir over a medium heat for a few minutes, then add a good glug of the milk and whisk to combine. Gradually add the rest of the milk, whisking in-between additions to get a smooth, creamy sauce. Stir in the Cheddar cheese, paprika and nutmeg and remove from the heat. Taste and add a little more salt and pepper, if you like.

Add the spinach into the sauce and, using a stick blender, blitz until smooth.

Cook the pasta for 2 minutes less than the instructions on the packet, then drain well. Tip into the green sauce and stir well until everything is combined.

Arrange the coated pasta in an ovenproof dish and scatter with the breadcrumbs and Parmesan cheese. Bake in the top of the oven for 20–25 minutes, until bubbling and golden on top.

CHEF'S NOTES

This sauce also makes an excellent cauliflower cheese. Chop your cauliflower into florets and blanch in boiling, salted water for 3 minutes, then drain and sit in a colander to allow the water to steam off (letting it dry ensures you won't end up with a watery dish). Tip the cauliflower into the baking dish, cover generously with the sauce and sprinkle with grated Cheddar, then bake as per the macaroni and cheese instructions.

JAKE, HEAD CHEF AT TOTTERIDGE SCHOOL

"Jake's energy is infectious – he is so young and political in his stance. When he joined us, he was our youngest head chef at a school. He went into a kitchen where staff had been doing things a certain way for years and ended up turning it around. Everyone loves going to work now. It's amazing how his incredible way with people came to shine. The kids are eating his food – and in volume. They take photos of before and after, and the plates are licked clean. He is working to change the food families eat every day of the week and teaching children the skills they need to make simple mid-week meals. Jake listens to the children. When they ask for things from the old menu, he will talk it through and find the middle ground – it's not just 'listen and give pizza', but it will be a pizza that fully meets the school food standards – for example with spelt flour and less salt. Jake teaches us the importance of listening and he also teaches me that patience is golden." Nicole

JAKE'S HERBY SPATCHCOCK CHICKEN

"During lockdown, when we had only 50 vulnerable or key worker students in school, we played around and made lots of exciting dishes for the kids. We had more time on our hands, so started ordering whole chickens in, and butchering ourselves to touch up on our butchery skills. This is one of the dishes we came up with and it was instantly a real hit with the students." Jake, School Head Chef, Totteridge Academy

Spatchcocking your chicken is a great way to speed up cooking time and give you a crispy skin. You also remove the backbone, which holds a lot of meat and flavour around it – this means you can start your stock/gravy/sauce much earlier than roasting the bird whole.

FEEDS 4-6

Zest and juice of 1 unwaxed lemon
6 garlic cloves, crushed
2 red chillies, roughly chopped
50ml/1¾fl oz extra virgin olive oil
50g/1¾oz capers
10–15 sprigs of thyme, leaves only
Small bunch of parsley, roughly
   chopped (including stalks)
Small bunch of coriander, roughly
   chopped (including stalks)
1 teaspoon cumin seeds
1 teaspoon coriander seeds
1 whole chicken, about 1.5kg/3lb 5oz
1 tablespoon sea salt

Add all your ingredients apart from the chicken and salt into the bowl of a food processor and blitz to a smooth paste. Depending on your equipment, you might need to do this in a couple of batches. If you don't have a food processor, you could chop finely and/or bash in a pestle and mortar.

Now it's time to 'spatchcock' your chicken. To do this, flip your bird over so its breast is on your chopping board and its legs are facing the front. Using a sharp knife (or scissors if you find this easier), cut along the right hand side of the back bone. Once you've done this side, cut along the left side. You should be able to remove the backbone as one piece, roughly an inch wide. Once removed, flip the chicken over so its breast is facing up and press quite firmly on the breast to flatten its ribs out.

Place your chicken in a bowl/tray and pour the herby mixture all over it, then leave to marinate for an hour at room temperature (or longer if you wish, in the fridge).

Before you want to cook your chicken, preheat your oven to its highest temperature. Place your chicken on a tray with the breast/skin facing up and sprinkle the sea salt on the skin. Roast for 25 minutes, then turn down to 170°C fan/190°C/375°F/gas mark 5 fan and roast for a further 20 minutes. Remove from the oven, and leave to rest for 10 minutes before carving.

Great with Maltese Potatoes (p. 114), Quinoa (p. 27) or Rice (p. 26) and Chilli Sauce (p. 29), or Salsa Verde (p. 30).

MACKEREL ON THE FIRE

We cook mackerel on the fire in our cooking lessons. We get the children to jump and dance around the fire, pretending to be cavemen. Mackerel is full of omega 3 oils, which keep the fish nice and moist and are full of health benefits. You know you've cracked this when the beautiful skin goes an amazing copper colour.

FEEDS 4

Olive oil
4 mackerel fillets
2 sprigs of rosemary
Sea salt and black pepper
Salsa Verde (p. 30), to serve

Prepare your fire; you want to be cooking over glowing embers. When the fire is hot, set a grill over it – making sure it's clean so your fish is less likely to stick to the bars – and brush with oil to prevent any further sticking. You can test the temperature is right by putting your hand above the grill and if you can't comfortably hold your hand over the fire and count for more than three seconds, it's ready.

Drizzle 1 tablespoon olive oil over the fish and generously rub seasoning into the skin. Place a couple of rosemary sprigs on the grill, purely for the smell of it. Arrange the fish on the grill, skin-side down.

The fish will take 4–6 minutes to cook on each side, depending on size. Don't worry if the skin tears; the fish will still taste amazing. Serve with Salsa Verde.

ANNA S ONE-PAN SqUASH, CAPER AND KALE PASTA

"It may not be for traditionalists, but I think this way of cooking pasta is clever – the starch from the pasta water comes together to make a velvety, creamy sauce that you wouldn't get if they were cooked separately. I'm not suggesting all pasta is cooked this way but, when a quick dinner is needed, this is where I look. You can swap in any pasta that cooks in about 8 minutes. I've gone for a wholewheat rigatoni, but I've had success with normal, quinoa and corn pasta too. I use Delicata squash, but you could use butternut squash instead – the skin is tougher, so it's best to peel it." Anna Jones, Chefs in Schools Supporter

FEEDS 6

1 small squash (about 400g/14oz), peeled if necessary
250g/9oz curly kale
2 tablespoons good olive oil
Pinch of sea salt
3 garlic cloves, finely chopped
350g/12oz pasta (I use wholewheat rigatoni or penne)
Zest of 2 unwaxed lemons
2 x 400g/14oz cans green lentils, drained
Pinch of dried chilli flakes
1 vegetable stock cube or 1 teaspoon vegetable bouillon powder
2 tablespoons baby capers, drained
50g/1¾oz Parmesan (I use a vegetarian one), grated

Peel your squash (if you are using butternut), then halve and scoop out the seeds. Thinly slice the squash halves into half-moons, about 5mm/¼ inch thick. Strip the kale leaves from their stalks and roughly tear any big pieces. Finely slice the stalks, discarding any particularly sinewy ones.

Heat a tablespoon of the olive oil in a large shallow pan over a medium heat and add the squash with a generous pinch of flaky sea salt. Cook the squash in the pan for about 10 minutes, stirring every couple of minutes, so that the pieces of squash start to catch and brown at the edges. Fill the kettle and put it on to boil.

Once the squash has had its 10 minutes, add the garlic and kale stalks and stir for a minute or so before adding the pasta, lemon zest, lentils, chilli, stock cube and 1 litre/1¾ pints of water from the kettle. Cover with a lid and cook on a medium heat for 6 minutes.

Next, remove the lid and add the kale leaves and capers. Cover with the lid for a couple more minutes, until the kale is starting to wilt and turn bright green. If your pasta is a little dry you can add a tiny bit more water, about 100ml/3½fl oz.

Remove the lid and simmer for another 2–3 minutes, until the water has been absorbed, then take the pan off the heat and stir through the remaining tablespoon of olive oil and half the Parmesan. Taste and add a little more salt if needed, then leave to sit for a minute or so before piling into bowls and topping with the remaining Parmesan.

BAKED HAKE

with Tomato Sauce

The beauty of this dish is that it's a school dinner that's sophisticated enough to serve at a dinner party. It's also one of the simplest in the book – particularly if you already have a batch of our tomato sauce in the freezer. Delicious also with the Maltese Potatoes on p. 114.

FEEDS 4

400ml/14fl oz Tomato and Miso
    Sauce (p. 31)
600g/1lb 5oz large hake fillet
Sea salt

Preheat the oven to 200°C fan/220°C/425°F/gas mark 7. Place your tomato sauce in the bottom of an oven tray and sit the hake on top, skin-side up. Season the hake with a scattering of sea salt.

Place the hake in the oven for 8 minutes. To check if it's ready, prod gently with a fork – it should feel firm.

Spoon between four plates and serve with the Maltese Potatoes (p. 114) or rice and roasted vegetables.

CHEF'S NOTES

This is a really great dinner-party dish. To add further interest, you could blacken thin slices of courgette on the griddle (pictured here) and layer between the potatoes and fish on a platter.

MIDW

"It's really hard to feed kids after school when you have 101 things to do at the same time – parents are superheroes at this time of day. These are all recipes that are quick to prepare, or they can be bulk-cooked and batched up into the freezer." NICOLE

EEK MEALS

Really? Again? It's often hard to believe that dinner has come around, already. Midweek is where cooking can become a real daily grind. Here, we hope you'll find inspiration as well as reliability; some take only the time it takes to boil up pasta, others can be made in advance and banged in the oven. This is not challenging food, either to make or to eat – yet it's not boring either. These dishes are the reliable friends of your kitchen: often easy enough to eat with a spoon, they're for those evenings when nothing but collapsing in front of the telly will do.

GREEN RISOTTO

This recipe is great for when you want the kids to eat something green. Because it is smooth and cheesy, it's much less challenging than leafy greens, which many children find tricky to approach.

FEEDS 4

1.2 litres/2 pints Basic Stock (p. 30)
2 tablespoons butter
2 tablespoons olive oil
1 onion, peeled and chopped
320g/11½oz risotto rice
200g/7oz baby spinach, fresh or defrosted
200g/7oz frozen peas
75ml/2½fl oz double cream
100g/3½oz Parmesan, finely grated
Grating of nutmeg
1 generous handful of fresh herbs e.g. parsley, basil, mint (optional)
Sea salt and black pepper
Extra virgin olive oil, to serve

CHEF'S NOTES

You can make double the volume of green paste and freeze half for next time.

Place the stock in a saucepan and heat until it is just short of boiling.

In a (flameproof) casserole or other heavy-based pan (which you'll use to make the risotto), melt the butter and oil and gently fry the onion until soft and translucent.

Add the rice and fry, stirring, to toast for a couple of minutes. Reduce the heat to low and start to add the stock, ladle by ladle, stirring from time to time. Don't let the rice get too thick or stodgy; instead, keep adding the stock. You do not need to stir constantly, just a few confident stirs every few minutes to make sure the rice isn't sticking to the pan.

Meanwhile, prepare the greens. If you are using frozen spinach, simply defrost and squeeze out the water. Have a big bowl of very cold, or better still, iced water ready. Bring a large pot of water to the boil, tip in the spinach, allow the water to return to the boil for 1 minute, then drain and plunge the leaves into the cold water. Allow to cool thoroughly, then squeeze out the water.

Place the drained spinach in a blender with the peas (still frozen is fine), a ladle of hot stock, the cream, half the Parmesan, the nutmeg and fresh herbs, if you are using them. Blitz to a paste, which can be as smooth or chunky as you like. Set aside.

When the risotto is almost ready and the rice still retains a slight bite, stir through the green paste. Cook for a couple of minutes, adding more stock, if necessary, to keep the texture you prefer (we like it soft and almost soupy).

Season with a few pinches of salt and black pepper and serve with the rest of the Parmesan and a swirl of your best olive oil over the top.

PASTA AL BURRO

with Broccoli

We like to use the whole vegetable wherever possible, and broccoli stalks are a much-overlooked ingredient. Peeled and cut into sticks, they make an excellent crudité, or are delicious shaved into a simple salad, dressed with olive oil and lemon. The greatest thing about this recipe is that kids actually prefer the broccoli stems to the broccoli as they provide a crunch to the pasta dish.

FEEDS 4

1 head broccoli (300g/10½oz)
400g/14oz penne pasta
50g/1¾oz unsalted butter
2 garlic cloves, peeled and finely chopped
½ teaspoon Urfa chilli flakes
½ teaspoon Aleppo chilli flakes
Sea salt and black pepper
50g/1¾oz Parmesan or Cheddar cheese, grated, to serve

First, cut the stalk off the broccoli and chop the head into bite-size florets. Peel the stalk and trim off the dry base, then cut into small dice.

Bring a large pot of water to the boil with a teaspoon of salt. Add the pasta and cook for 9–10 minutes, until al dente.

Meanwhile, in a medium saucepan (for which you have a lid), melt 30g/1oz of the butter and add the diced broccoli stalk. Cook for 5 minutes, then add the florets and cook for another 3 minutes. Add the garlic and chilli flakes, season with salt and pepper and cook for a further 5 minutes with the lid on.

Drain the pasta, reserving 2 tablespoons of the cooking water, and add to the broccoli along with the remaining butter. Stir to mix and season again to taste. Serve with grated Parmesan or Cheddar.

CHEF'S NOTES

We have specified two types of particularly lovely, aromatic chilli flakes – Urfa and Aleppo – but you can substitute with regular chilli flakes (which will be hotter so reduce the quantity a little), or experiment with others, such as chipotle, which would give a smoky flavour.

ORANGE PASTA

The children love playful names for dishes. We sometimes call fish without breadcrumbs 'Naked Fish' and pasta with carrot and butternut squash 'Orange Pasta'. It makes them giggle. This might not seem easy to make on a whim but, made in bulk, it is easy to freeze in portions and then, when you need a meal in minutes, all you have to do is boil the pasta.

FEEDS 12

3 carrots, peeled and roughly chopped

3 small sweet potatoes, peeled and roughly chopped

½ butternut squash, peeled and roughly chopped

Olive oil, for drizzling

3 tablespoons coconut oil

2 red onions, peeled and finely sliced

2 garlic cloves, peeled and finely chopped

1 litre/1¾ pints vegetable stock

200ml/7fl oz passata

1 x 400ml/14fl oz can coconut milk

2 teaspoons sea salt

100g/3½oz spaghetti per person (or other pasta)

50g/1¾oz grated cheese, to serve (optional)

Preheat the oven to 200ºC fan/220ºC/425ºF/gas mark 7.

Tip the carrot, sweet potato and butternut squash onto a couple of large oven trays, drizzle with olive oil and roast until tender and beginning to bronze, about 30 minutes.

Meanwhile, in a large saucepan (for which you have a lid), heat the coconut oil over a medium heat. When hot, add the onion and garlic and fry until soft and translucent, about 10 minutes.

When the veg has finished roasting, carefully tip them into the pan with the onions and add the vegetable stock, passata, coconut milk and 1 teaspoon of the salt. Cover with a lid and simmer gently for 1 hour.

Meanwhile, bring a large pot of water to the boil with the remaining salt. Add the spaghetti or pasta of your choice and cook for 9–10 minutes, until al dente, then drain.

Using a stick blender, blitz the sauce until smooth. Heap the pasta into bowls, spoon over the sauce and serve with grated cheese, if you like.

FISH MOILEE

This wonderful Keralan curry is so quick to put together that it can be an everyday dinner as well as a good option for entertaining. To make it vegetarian, omit the fish and double the amount of sweet potato.

FEEDS 4

1 teaspoon black mustard seeds

8 curry leaves (dried is fine)

1 cinnamon stick

2 tablespoons coconut oil

2 onions, peeled and finely chopped

2 garlic cloves, peeled and finely chopped

5-cm/2-inch piece of fresh ginger, peeled and grated

Pinch of chilli flakes

1 tablespoon ground cumin

1 teaspoon ground turmeric

2 x 400ml/14fl oz cans coconut milk

½ teaspoon salt

1 tablespoon white wine vinegar

2 medium sweet potatoes, peeled and cubed

300g/10½oz fish – one type or mixed (e.g. 200g/7oz salmon, 100g/3½oz smoked haddock or frozen North Atlantic prawns), cubed as you would for a fish pie

12 cherry tomatoes

TO SERVE
Cooked basmati rice, from p. 26
Fresh herbs, to garnish

First, in a large sauté or deep frying pan placed over a low heat, dry-fry the black mustard seeds, curry leaves and cinnamon stick until the mustard seeds start to pop. Stir in the oil and add the onion, then fry gently until soft and translucent, about 5 minutes.

Add the garlic and ginger, chilli, cumin and turmeric and continue to fry until the onion is just starting to turn golden. Add the coconut milk, salt and vinegar and simmer for 5 minutes. All this can be prepared ahead of time and reheated when necessary.

Add your sweet potato and simmer for 10 minutes until just soft to the tip of a knife. Finally, gently lower in the fish and the cherry tomatoes and simmer for 5 minutes until just cooked.

Serve with rice and garnish with whatever fresh herbs you have to hand.

PRAWN TOAST

"This brings back a beautiful memory for me and I still love to make them for most of my friends' children as an easy meal. It always goes down well and puts a smile on my face." Nicole

FEEDS 4

4 slices of bread

165g/5¾oz raw prawns, roughly chopped

1 free-range egg, white and yolk separated

1 tablespoon plus 1 teaspoon soy sauce

1 tablespoon toasted sesame oil

1 tablespoon sesame seeds, black or white or both

TO SERVE

Soy sauce or chilli sauce, from p. 29

Preheat the oven to 220°C fan/240°C/475°F/gas mark 9 and line a large oven tray with a baking mat or baking paper.

Place the sliced bread on the baking tray and toast lightly and evenly on each side.

In a jug, combine the prawns, egg white, soy sauce and sesame oil and, using a stick blender, blitz to a smooth paste. Spread a quarter of the mixture on each slice of bread, being careful that it doesn't spill over the edges. Return the tray to the oven and bake for 8–10 minutes, until the mixture has turned pink and is firm to the touch.

In the meantime, tip the sesame seeds into a bowl and get a pastry brush ready for the egg yolk. When the prawn toasts are cooked, remove from the oven and brush the pink prawn mixture of one of the slices with a little egg yolk, then liberally sprinkle with sesame seeds. You'll need to work quickly, as the egg yolk will dry quite quickly, meaning the sesame seeds won't stick. Repeat with the remaining slices of toast.

Using a serrated knife, diagonally cut each slice of prawn toast into quarters and place back on the baking tray. Return the tray to the oven for a final 5 minutes, then serve immediately.

DHAL

Dhal is a regular on most of our menus. It's delicious, nutritious, planet-friendly and cheap, which allows us to balance the budget and spend more on other dishes during the week.

FEEDS 4

400g/14oz red lentils
2 teaspoons ground turmeric
2 teaspoons ground ginger
50g/1¾oz unsalted butter
Juice of 1 lemon
1 teaspoon coconut oil
100g/3½oz baby spinach
Sea salt
Plain yogurt, to serve (optional)

FOR THE TEMPER
2 tablespoons groundnut oil
1 tablespoon cumin seeds
1 teaspoon chilli flakes, or to taste
1 teaspoon black onion seeds
2 shallots, peeled and finely sliced

Rinse the lentils well and tip into a large saucepan (for which you have a lid) along with 1 litre/1¾ pints water, then place over a medium heat. Add the turmeric and ginger, put the lid on and bring to the boil, then reduce the heat to a simmer until the lentils are breaking apart, about 20–30 minutes.

Take the pan off the heat and add 1½ teaspoons salt, the butter and lemon juice. Stir the pot once, put the lid back on and set aside while you make the temper.

In a small frying pan, heat the groundnut oil and add the cumin seeds, chilli flakes and black onion seeds. Toss for about 30 seconds until they colour and release their aromas. Add the shallots and fry until golden and crispy. Spoon into a bowl and set aside.

Place the pan back on the heat with the coconut oil and add the spinach and a good pinch of salt. Sauté until the spinach wilts, just a minute or so.

Serve the dhal with the crispy spiced shallot and sautéed spinach on top. A spoonful of yogurt also works very well, if you like.

SPECIAL FRIED RICE

Nasi goreng is an Indonesian fried rice that is very popular, very versatile and a great way to use up leftover rice and vegetables. To make it a complete dinner, serve with a fried egg on top of each portion, sunny-side up.

FEEDS 4

400g/14oz rice
1 tablespoon soy sauce
2 teaspoons toasted sesame oil
4 free-range eggs
20g/¾oz unsalted butter
6 spring onions, topped, tailed and finely sliced
1.5-cm/⅓-inch piece of fresh ginger, peeled and grated
2 heads of broccoli, cut into bite-size florets, stem peeled and roughly chopped
150g/5½oz peeled prawns or leftover chicken, optional
75g/2¾oz frozen peas

FOR THE DRESSING
1 tablespoon sugar
1 tablespoon soy sauce
1.5-cm/⅓-inch piece of fresh ginger, peeled and grated
2 garlic cloves, peeled and grated
2 tablespoons toasted sesame oil
2 tablespoons rice vinegar

Follow the instructions for cooking rice on p. 26. When it comes to turning off the heat, add the tablespoon of soy sauce and put the lid back on, to allow the rice to steam.

Now, heat the sesame oil in a large frying pan until very hot. Break in the eggs, stirring to break them up, and cook, stirring frequently, so that they break down into small omelette-like pieces. Once fully cooked and starting to colour, scrape out of the pan and set aside.

In the same pan, melt the butter over a medium heat, add the spring onion and ginger and cook for a couple of minutes. Add the broccoli along with a splash of water, cover with a lid and simmer for 3 minutes. Add the prawns and peas to the onions and toss gently. Reduce the heat to low for 3–5 minutes, and cook until the prawns are pink.

To make the dressing, combine all the ingredients in a small bowl and stir to dissolve the sugar.

Now turn up the heat again under the frying pan. Add the rice and egg back into the pan and stir until thoroughly combined and hot throughout. Pour over the dressing, stir through carefully, then divide between plates or serve on a platter in the middle of the table.

OLI, SCHOOL CHEF TRAINER AND FORMER SCHOOL HEAD CHEF

"I worked with Oli at NOPI and can honestly say that Chefs in Schools would not have taken off if it weren't for him. He allowed me to dream how far we could take the project. He brought a lot of the food ideas, recipes from NOPI that we adapted, and the Edible Garden is also one of them (see page 110). He made breaded mussels – 4,000–5,000 of them – for the kids. It took from 7 a.m. to midday and was hard work but exciting for us. Yet the hard work does not always pay off. We tried a beetroot curry and a dish of rolled pasta, based on a NOPI recipe – it was too much! The children had never seen anything like it before. They wouldn't eat it and we were very upset – both dishes took three days to make. Oli still teaches me things everyday but has taught me a vital rule for Chefs in Schools – do not run before you can walk. If you're doing a recipe that takes three days – make sure the children will eat it! You must put the foundations in first."
Nicole

SOUSOU'S MOROCCAN CHICKEN

"We make this dish at Gayhurst week after week and the children love it. Every time I make it at another school, it reminds of me of SouSou and her amazing cooking." Nicole

FEEDS 6

3 tablespoons olive oil

2 red onions, peeled and sliced

2 cinnamon sticks

1 tablespoon ground cumin

1 tablespoon ground turmeric

12 pieces of chicken (leg and thigh), skin on and bone in

30g/1oz preserved lemon, pulp discarded and skin finely sliced

2 star anise

500ml/18fl oz chicken stock

200g/7oz green olives, pitted

TO SERVE
½ teaspoon salt

Handful of fresh herbs, optional

Preheat the oven to 150°C fan/170°C/340°F/gas mark 3½.

Place a (flameproof) casserole over a medium heat, add the olive oil and, when hot, fry the onion along with the cinnamon, cumin and turmeric. Cook for 2–3 minutes until the spices smell fragrant, then add the chicken, turning occasionally until all the pieces take on a good golden colour.

Add the preserved lemon, star anise and chicken stock and stir to combine. Bring to the boil, cover and place in the oven for 45 minutes. After this time, switch the oven off, then add the olives and place the pot back in the oven to rest for 20 minutes before serving.

Season with a little salt, sprinkle with fresh herbs (optional) and serve with couscous (p. 28).

TuMMI'S CRISPIEST-EVER CHICKEN THIGHS *with Broccoli*

"So crispy that you would think that they were deep-fried; so simple that you could make them with your eyes shut; so popular with children, hot out of the pan, that this is a recipe that I use repeatedly for feeding my gang and their friends. They can even help cook them." Thomasina Miers, Chefs in Schools Trustee

FEEDS 4-8, DEPENDING ON APPETITES

8 bone-in, skin-on chicken thighs
1 tablespoon olive oil
200g/7oz cherry tomatoes
4 tablespoons sherry or dry
   white wine
Juice and zest of 1 unwaxed lemon
1 broccoli, head cut into florets and
   inner stalk trimmed and cubed
Sea salt and black pepper
Lemon wedges, to serve

Season the chicken thighs generously on both sides and set aside for 15 minutes while they reach room temperature.

Heat a large, heavy-based frying pan over a medium heat and, when hot, add the oil, followed by the thighs, skin-side down. Fry for 20–25 minutes, draining the fat into a heatproof pot every 10 minutes or so and checking the colour of the skin – if it looks as if it is colouring too quickly, turn the heat down a little.

Once the skin is crisp and deep golden, turn the thighs over, add the cherry tomatoes and sherry, plus half the lemon juice and zest and cook on the other side for 10–15 minutes, or until the chicken juices run completely clear.

Bring a saucepan of water to the boil and steam the broccoli for 6–8 minutes, then add to the pan with the remaining lemon juice. Flip the chicken thighs over onto their skins to warm and then serve scattered with the rest of the lemon zest.

CHEF'S NOTES

Chopped preserved lemon and green olives are a great way to add more complex flavours to this dish (pictured here). Add to the pan in place of the cherry tomatoes.

LEuN MEATBALLs

Allegra McEvedy is such an inspiring chef. Co-presenter of CBBC's kids cooking show *Step Up to the Plate*, she's long been committed to brilliant food for kids. She teaches at her daughter's school and works with contract caterers to improve their food in schools. This recipe is adapted from one by Allegra in her cookbook *Leon*.

FEEDS 6

1 wholemeal pitta or leftover flatbread, ripped into small pieces (you could also use leftover bread or breadcrumbs here)

4 tablespoons milk

500g/1lb 2oz minced lamb

2 tablespoons parsley, finely chopped

2 tablespoons mint, finely chopped

1 teaspoon dried oregano

1 garlic clove, peeled and minced

½ teaspoon sea salt

Olive oil, for drizzling

1½ batches Tomato and Miso Sauce (p. 31)

1 tablespoon rose harissa or harissa (optional)

TO SERVE

Flatbread (p. 122)

Brown rice, quinoa (p. 27) or couscous (p. 28)

Fresh herbs, optional

Preheat the oven to 160ºC fan/180ºC/350ºF/gas mark 4.

In a medium bowl, add the pieces of pitta, pour over the milk and leave to soak for 10 minutes. After this time, add the mince, herbs, garlic and salt and mix well with your hands.

Roll the mixture into balls about the size of a ping pong ball (approx. 25g/1oz) and arrange them on an oven tray. Drizzle with a little olive oil and bake in the oven until golden brown and cooked through, about 15–20 minutes.

Meanwhile, add the tomato sauce to a large pan and stir through the harissa, if you are using it. Warm it through and, when the meatballs are ready, carefully add to the sauce and simmer together for a few minutes.

Serve with flatbread and brown rice or couscous, and any fresh herbs you have to hand, if you like.

CHEF'S NOTES

To take these in a more Italian direction, replace the lamb mince with beef, pork or a mixture of both, and replace the mint with basil. Finally, scent the tomato sauce with basil instead of harissa and eat with spaghetti, topped with a generous grating of Parmesan.

To start the journey for kids shy of strong flavours, leave out the harissa from the sauce to start with, and gradually add a little more each time to get used to the new flavour.

Leftovers are delicious stuffed into toasted pitta bread with a crunchy chopped salad and gherkins.

STRE
AND

"*Food has always been a part of my life. When I was growing up in Jeda, Saudi Arabia, my family had a restaurant and I spent a lot of time there. One of the chefs, Jamal, showed me how to make samosas. I learned from watching him. The school children always ask for them as they love them. For me, it takes about half an hour to make 200 but I am used it – it's so easy! They are fiddly but it is good to learn new things.*"
SAMIA, SCHOOL SOUS CHEF

ET FOOD SNACKS

Several of the most inspiring chefs we work with come from a street food background, and we've found that offering kids – particularly teens – street-style food is a great way to engage them with new food and earn their trust. Since secondary school kids can vote with their feet and with their pockets, it's a crucial step in the journey to change. In order to get their custom (and to know that they're not wasting their money or their health on low-grade fast food), we needed to compete with what was available on the street corner: it had to be chew-your-fist tasty, it had to be cheap – and it had to be a bit sexy. These recipes offer a window into the current youth food trends (a world of shipping-container restaurants and music festivals), all adapted for the home kitchen.

CORN RIBS

These corn ribs are such a fun way to get kids to enjoy corn on the cob – you gnaw on them like beavers – and adults and children alike love them. In fact, they're such fun, this might well be our favourite recipe in the whole book.

FEEDS 4, AS A STARTER OR SNACK

5 tablespoons coconut oil

2 corn cobs, husks removed

4 tablespoons garlic mayonnaise (aioli)

½ teaspoon chilli flakes (or to taste)

1 lime, squeezed to get 2 teaspoons juice

Sea salt

TO SERVE

20g/¾oz finely grated cheese, like Cheddar

Fresh herbs/micro leaves and sliced spring onions, optional

1 lime, cut into wedges

Preheat the oven to 220°C fan/240°C/475°F/gas mark 9. Place a roasting tray with the coconut oil in the oven to heat up.

Bring a pan of water to the boil. Slice each corn cob in half crossways and blanch in the pan for 5 minutes, then refresh in a bowl of iced water. Drain thoroughly on kitchen paper to dry and then quarter the corn lengthways. You should have 16 pieces of corn.

Prepare a large plate, lined with kitchen paper for the corn to drain on.

Carefully take the hot tray of oil from the oven and add the corn, returning it to the oven as quickly as possible. Roast for 10 minutes, basting halfway through.

Meanwhile, in a small bowl, whisk together the aioli, chilli flakes and lime juice.

When the corn has curled up, remove from the oven and drain on the paper-lined plate. Season with salt and toss with the spicy aioli.

Transfer the corn ribs to a fresh plate, sprinkle over the grated cheese, herbs/micro leaves and spring onions and serve with fresh lime wedges.

SUMMER ROLLS

Hot smoked salmon is a luxury but it adds such a bang of flavour that a little goes a long way. These rolls are light and have a real freshness about them – they're a great home for any leftovers, too, such as chicken or strips of omelette.

FEEDS 4 (MAKES 8 ROLLS)

8 rice paper wrappers
2 tablespoons mayonnaise
Handful of baby spinach leaves
200g/7oz hot smoked salmon, leftover chicken or smoked tofu, chopped
1 carrot, grated
1 spring onion, very finely sliced
Fresh herbs or micro herbs, optional

FOR THE DIPPING SAUCE
2 teaspoons coconut sugar (or soft brown sugar)
1 lime, juiced to get 2 teaspoons
1 teaspoon fish sauce
1 garlic clove, peeled and minced
1 green chilli, very finely sliced

First make the dipping sauce; mix all the ingredients together in a small bowl and set aside.

Make sure you have all the components for the rolls ready as they will come together very quickly. Fill a large lipped plate or shallow bowl with tepid water and clear a space on your worktop.

Dip a rice paper wrapper in the water for 2 seconds, making sure it gets fully submerged. Give it a good shake to remove any excess water, then lay on the worktop and repeat with the remaining wrappers.

Place a small spoonful of mayonnaise onto each wrapper, followed by a few spinach leaves, a little spring onion and fresh herbs (optional) and 2 tablespoons each of salmon and grated carrot. Fold one edge of the wrapper over the filling, fold in the ends and then roll up the rice paper wrapper tightly to enclose the filling. Repeat the folding process with the remaining rolls, then transfer to a serving plate, alongside the dipping sauce.

If you're not going to eat the rolls straight away, cover them with a clean, damp cloth so they don't dry out, and keep in the fridge if storing for more than 1 hour.

SAMIA, SOUS CHEF, MANDEVILLE PRIMARY SCHOOL

"Samia was in the kitchen when I arrived and I spotted her straight away, because when you enter a space you instinctively see who has skills. Samia was amazing with her hands: gyoza, samosas and fritters – she could do them at speed. She is a strong person and made me feel like I was in a normal kitchen when I was getting used to working in a school. When I arrived, the team were cooking Toad in the Hole and Roast Beef. No matter how good you are, if it's out of your comfort zone it's a struggle, so I started to ask what they wanted to cook. I wanted to involve everyone in the process of changing the menu and so we talked about food they'd like to see. As soon as we started cooking the food they enjoyed making at home – curries, samosas, jollof rice – an amazing repertoire of skills opened up, which hadn't been used at the school before. I found out that Samia could do an amazing basbousa cake. We added custard to it and it became the best thing on the menu." Nicole

SAMIA'S SAMOSAS

Making the quick fresh mango chutney really adds a hit of freshness and fragrance. Otherwise, a squeeze of lime stirred into a jar of shop-bought mango chutney really helps. You can make these samosas in advance or make a huge batch and freeze them.

This recipe is on the following page

SAMIA'S SAMOSAS

MAKES 20

2 tablespoons rapeseed oil, plus extra for glazing
½ onion, peeled and roughly chopped
1 carrot, peeled and roughly chopped
1 beetroot, peeled and roughly chopped
½ teaspoon chilli powder
1 teaspoon mustard powder
4 teaspoons ground coriander
Sea salt
100g/3½oz frozen peas, defrosted
1 x 220g/7½oz pack filo pastry
Rapeseed oil, for brushing

In a frying pan over a medium heat, add the oil and, when hot, add the onion and cook until soft and translucent, about 10 minutes. Add the carrot, beetroot, spices and ½ teaspoon of salt and cook until the vegetables are soft, around 10 minutes, stirring to make sure the spices don't catch. Set aside to cool.

Tip the mixture into a food processor and pulse briefly to break down the vegetables into pea-size pieces. Add the defrosted peas, stir to mix, then clear a space on your worktop to assemble the samosas.

Preheat the oven to 180°C fan/200°C/400°F/gas mark 6 and line an oven tray with baking paper.

Take a sheet of filo, lay it on your worktop with the pointed side facing you and cover the other sheets with a slightly damp towel (to stop them drying out).

Place a heaped tablespoon of filling at the bottom of the sheet, and fold the bottom right corner over the filling, so it meets the left edge. Repeat with the bottom right corner and keep going up the pastry sheet until you have a neat little triangle.

Put the samosa on the lined tray and repeat until you have used up all the filling.

Brush the samosas with a little rapeseed oil and bake in the oven until golden brown, around 15 minutes.

CHEF'S NOTES

To make a quick fresh chutney, blitz together the flesh of a mango, a 2-cm/1-inch piece of fresh ginger, 1 red chilli, 2 teaspoons lime juice and a big pinch of salt and pepper until smooth. Taste for seasoning, adding 1 tablespoon honey if your mango isn't sweet enough.

HELEN'S VEGGIE SAUSAGE ROLLS

If you just call these 'sausage rolls', we'd be surprised if anyone noticed there was no meat. For a vegan version, omit the egg wash and replace the Cheddar with a tablespoon of miso paste.

MAKES 8 VEGGIE SAUSAGE ROLLS, OR 16 SMALL ONES

2 tablespoons olive oil
1 red onion, peeled and roughly chopped
1 carrot, peeled and roughly chopped
1 stick of celery, roughly chopped
½ teaspoon salt
150g/5½oz chestnut mushrooms, roughly chopped
1 x 400g/14oz can green lentils, drained
50g/1¾oz breadcrumbs
100g/3½oz Cheddar, grated
1 free-range egg, beaten
1 x 320g/11½oz pack ready-rolled puff pastry
2 tablespoons black sesame seeds

In a frying pan, heat the oil over a medium heat and, when hot, add the onion, carrot, celery and salt and cook until soft, around 10 minutes. Add the mushrooms and cook until they have reduced in size and any liquid has evaporated. Add the lentils to the pan, stir and take off the heat to allow to cool.

Preheat the oven to 160°C fan/180°C/350°F/gas mark 4 and prepare an oven tray with a reusable baking mat.

Once cool, tip the mixture into a large bowl and use a stick blender to blitz to a rough paste. Stir through the breadcrumbs and Cheddar. Take out 1 tablespoon of the beaten egg mix and set aside to glaze the sausage rolls with later. Add the rest of the egg to the veg mixture and stir well to combine.

Lay the pastry out on your worktop, with the long side facing you, and cut in half across the middle, so you have two long pieces of pastry. Scoop the mixture out of the bowl and divide evenly between the two pieces of pastry, moulding it into a long sausage shape, running along the centre of each piece. Fold the top half of the pastry over the mix, so it meets the other edge, lifting the bottom edge up to meet it. Use a fork to crimp the edges together and repeat with the other piece of pastry so you have two long sausage shapes.

Brush the pastry with the remaining egg, and sprinkle with black sesame seeds. Cut each log into four pieces so you have eight sausage rolls in total, and place them on the lined baking tray, spaced evenly apart. Bake for 30–35 minutes until the pastry has puffed up and is a deep golden colour. Allow to cool a little before eating warm, or at room temperature.

DAVID'S CHICKEN LOLLIPOPS

Head Chef David Darmanin created this recipe to entice suspicious pupils of a secondary school in Hounslow when he first started working with us. It was a hit and has been on many school menus since. You'll need to begin this recipe a day ahead in order to marinate the chicken, and you'll also need some wooden skewers for the lollipops. It's great served with the Corn Salad (p. 114) on the side.

FEEDS 4-6 (MAKES ABOUT 12 LOLLIPOPS)

500g/1lb 2oz chicken thighs, cut into 5cm x 2cm (2in x 1in) strips
Olive oil, for drizzling

FOR THE MARINADE
300ml/10½fl oz buttermilk
1½ teaspoons Dijon mustard
¼ teaspoon cayenne pepper
¼ teaspoon salt
Cracked black pepper

FOR THE COATING
75g/2¾oz rice flour
75g/2¾oz corn flour
1 teaspoon cracked black pepper
1½ teaspoons ground coriander
1 teaspoon garlic powder
¼ teaspoon cayenne pepper
1 teaspoon dried oregano
¾ teaspoon celery or onion salt

The day before you want to eat, put all the ingredients for the marinade in a large tub (for which you have a lid). Stir well, then add the chicken pieces and turn until the chicken is completely coated. Put the lid on and refrigerate until the following day.

Preheat the oven to 220°C fan/240°C/475°F/gas mark 9. Line a large oven tray with a baking mat and drizzle with a little olive oil. Take the chicken out of the fridge.

In a deep-sided tray (or large lipped plate), mix all the ingredients for the coating together.

Carefully lift the chicken pieces from the marinade and arrange on a plate, then discard the marinade. Get another plate ready to put the coated chicken pieces on and have your skewers at the ready.

Take a piece of chicken, dredge it in the floury coating and then place on the clean plate. Repeat with the remaining pieces of chicken. Next, take a skewer and insert the sharp end into the thigh, lengthways. If your piece of chicken is longer than your skewer, you can fold the chicken, like a concertina.

Place the skewers on the oven tray, drizzle with a little oil and bake for 15 minutes, turning the skewers over halfway through cooking, until golden brown and the chicken is cooked through. Serve hot from the oven, with the corn salad.

ANCHOVY CHEESE STRAWS

This is a luxury snack or great party food and we recommend you eat them warm, straight from the oven. The anchovy provides that umami taste which the children are in love with – salty, sour, bitter, fatty and sweet all at the same time. Using anchovy blitzed and brushed onto the puff pastry means that kids are not aware of what it is, and can just appreciate the flavour addition.

MAKES 12

100g/3½oz butter
3 anchovy fillets
Plain flour, for dusting
375g/13oz puff pastry sheet
70g/2½oz mature Cheddar, grated
2 teaspoons black sesame seeds

Preheat the oven to 180°C fan/200°C/400°F/gas mark 6.

Place the butter and anchovies in a food processor and blitz until smooth.

Dust your clean kitchen worktop with a little flour. Lay out the pastry and brush with three-quarters of the butter mix, then sprinkle over all the cheese. Fold the sheet in half and then roll it out to its original size, then fold into four and roll this piece again back to the original size.

Spread with the remaining butter and sprinkle with sesame seeds. Slice in half horizontally, then cut into long strips about 1cm/½ inch wide. With each strip, hold one end still while twisting the other end to form a twirl.

Arrange on a baking tray lined with baking paper and cook in the oven for 10 minutes until golden brown.

JACOB AND SAM, 'THE WOODY BOYS' - WOODMANSTERNE SCHOOL

"We were looking for a new chef for Woodmansterne, our first school with older pupils. Jacob (pictured left) came in for a trial; we threw an apron at him, he rolled up his sleeves and got stuck in. His best friend Sam (on the right) worked with him on a street food business – Luxury Flats – and they started to share the Head Chef role. It was exciting to see them push boundaries. They were always thinking, 'What's exciting about food?' and 'How can I serve it to kids?' They are building a food-smoking cupboard, a snack shack, and plan to create a restaurant. They serve tasting plates and sharing platters to the children – razor clams and mussels, bao buns, hake fritters with sauce gribiche, chicken liver bánh mì (a Vietnamese baguette). They have fun with school food and dream big. I've done school food for a long time and sometimes it's easy to anticipate what can go wrong. However, I only have to look at how they work to remember that anything is possible." Nicole

THE WOODY BOYS' EDAMAME FALAFEL

Before joining Woodmansterne School, Jake and Sam ran a flatbread business called 'Luxury Flats' that sold street food at festivals. Their bestseller was this bright green and vibrant-tasting edamame falafel, which they would make by the thousand.

FEEDS ABOUT 8

750g/1lb 10oz frozen shelled edamame beans, defrosted

1 x 400g/14oz can chickpeas, drained with liquid reserved

½ bunch of coriander

4 spring onions, trimmed and roughly chopped

8 garlic cloves, peeled and roughly chopped

1 litre/1¾ pints rapeseed oil

5 tablespoons gram flour

Sea salt and black pepper

TO SERVE

Flatbread (p. 122) or pitta
Salad
Hummus
Yogurt
Hot sauce

Place the edamame, chickpeas, coriander, spring onion and garlic in a blender along with 1 teaspoon of salt and ½ teaspoon pepper and whizz it all up until it makes a sort of chunky hummus. At this point it's delicious as a dip! Tip into a large bowl while you prepare the oil.

Place the oil either in a deep-fat fryer, set at 180°C/350°F, or in a deep saucepan over a medium-high heat and bring to a gentle simmer.

To continue making the falafel, add 2 tablespoons of the reserved chickpea liquid to the mix along with the gram flour and stir to combine. The mixture should start to clump together. If it's still a little wet, add a little more flour.

Take some of the mixture and roll it to the size of a meatball, then drop it into the hot oil to make sure it is bound properly and does not break up. If it breaks up, add a bit more flour to the mixture. Roll the remaining mixture into meatball-sized falafels.

Fry the falafel in batches for 3–5 minutes, then lift out with a slotted spoon and transfer to a plate lined with kitchen paper to soak up any excess grease. Sprinkle with a little salt.

Serve this in a flatbread or pitta with salad, hummus, yogurt and hot sauce. Or have it atop a tomato salad with feta and olives. Or simply serve it as it is... the possibilities are endless.

GYOZA

One of the kids' favourite cooking lessons is making gyoza and they are a fun joint project. It's a flexible recipe – you can fill them with pretty much anything: a good place for a small amount of leftover chicken, for example.

MAKES 30 DUMPLINGS

Rapeseed oil

½ white cabbage (about 250g/9oz), cored and finely sliced

100g/1¾oz shiitake mushrooms, finely sliced

3-cm/1¼-inch piece of fresh ginger, peeled and finely chopped

1 teaspoon sea salt

1 tablespoon soy sauce

30 gyoza wrappers, defrosted if frozen

Soy sauce or chilli Sauce (p. 29), to serve

In a frying pan (for which you have a lid), heat 2 tablespoons of oil and, when hot, add the cabbage, shiitake, ginger and salt and fry until the cabbage has softened and the vegetables are beginning to caramelise. Stir through the soy sauce, then take off the heat and set aside to cool.

When cool, tip the filling into a bowl and wipe the pan out, but don't wash it out – you'll cook the gyoza in this later.

When you're ready to assemble the gyoza, fill a small bowl with water, and have it handy. Take one gyoza wrapper in the palm of one hand and place a tablespoon (15g/½oz) of the filling in the centre. Dip your finger in the bowl of water and run it along half of the edge of the wrapper, then fold together to form a half moon shape. Pinch the edges firmly shut. If you'd like to pleat the edges, make small folds along the top curved edge of the gyoza wrapper, pinching them hard to keep them in place.

When you're ready to cook the gyoza, heat 1 tablespoon oil in the frying pan over a medium-high heat. When hot, add ten gyoza to the pan, arranging them on their sides, and fry for 2 minutes. Don't turn them over – you just want one crispy side. After 2 minutes, add 2 tablespoons of water to the pan and quickly put the lid on, so they can steam for another 3 minutes. After this time, lift the gyoza onto a plate and continue cooking the rest. Serve with chilli sauce on the side.

FEA

"When the opportunity came up to work with a great chef on improving school food at one of my schools, I jumped at it. Better nutrition and happier lunches were my first objectives but, once I started working with Nicole, it became about so much more. I love the theatre she brings to school food, such as having pea shoots on the table along with children's scissors so that they can snip some shoots and add them to their food."
LOUISE, EXECUTIVE HEAD OF LEAP FEDERATION

STING

Every school dinner is a feast. There's little as symbolic as a significant gathering around food – whether that's for a hallmark holiday or just because it's a weekend, the sun is out, and, well, you can. Every culture gathers around food to mark a moment, and most of these recipes come directly out of the home kitchens of our school chefs. Sharing food from each other's cultures is a bridge to so many other connections. Whether it's SouSou's Burek, Toni's Jollof Rice or Sara's Ethiopian Chicken, these are family recipes from around the world that come to you via our schools.

SWEET PuTaTu CHaaT cURRY

Placed in the centre of the table or individually plated, this is one for treating your family.

FEEDS 6

5 tablespoons olive oil

1 onion, peeled and roughly chopped

2-cm/1-inch piece of fresh ginger, peeled and roughly chopped

4 garlic cloves, peeled and roughly chopped

½ stick of lemongrass, roughly chopped

2 tablespoons tomato purée

1 tablespoon rose harissa

1 teaspoon mild curry powder

1 red chilli (optional)

1 x 400ml/14fl oz can coconut milk

Sea salt

½ cauliflower, cut into bite-size florets

¼ butternut squash (about 200g/7oz), peeled and cut into 2-cm/1-inch slices

2 sweet potatoes (about 400g/14oz), peeled and cut into 3-cm/1-inch chunks

1 x 400g/14oz can chickpeas, drained (or 250g/9oz frozen cooked chickpeas)

TO GARNISH

Handful of fresh coriander, roughly chopped

2 spring onions, sliced at an angle

Preheat the oven to 220ºC fan/240ºC/475ºF/gas mark 9.

To make the curry sauce, heat 2 tablespoons of the olive oil in a medium saucepan (for which you have a lid) and cook the onion over a low heat until soft and translucent. Add the ginger, garlic, lemongrass, tomato purée, harissa, curry powder and chilli, if using, and stir to combine. Cook for 5 minutes, stirring frequently to make sure it doesn't catch, and then add the coconut milk with ¾ teaspoon salt. Place the lid on, turn the heat down to a simmer and cook for 30 minutes.

Meanwhile, in a large bowl, mix together the cauliflower, butternut squash and sweet potato with the remaining oil, until the veg is nicely coated. Sprinkle over ½ teaspoon salt, mix again and tip into an oven tray. Roast for 15–20 minutes, until the vegetables are just tender and beginning to burnish.

When the sauce has finished cooking, take it off the heat and blitz until smooth with a stick blender. Tip in the chickpeas, stir and place back on a low heat to warm the chickpeas through. Remove the roasted veg from the oven.

To serve, spoon the sauce and chickpeas into shallow bowls, top with the roasted veg and sprinkle over the chopped coriander and spring onion to garnish.

SOUSOU'S BUREK

Burek, a type of baked, filled pastry made with a delicate filo-like dough, date back to the days of the Ottoman Empire, when they would be the centrepiece of Sultan Mehmed's daily feasts. Traditionally filled with feta, spinach and chicken, they are endlessly adaptable and ever-popular. Here we have used puff pastry, which is easier to handle and more substantial. You can serve with warm yogurt, if you like.

FEEDS 4

2 tablespoons olive oil, plus extra for brushing

1 red onion, peeled and diced

250g/9oz frozen spinach, defrosted and excess liquid squeezed out

½ teaspoon paprika

½ teaspoon salt

200g/7oz feta

½ x 375g pack ready-rolled puff pastry

1 tablespoon black sesame seeds

Preheat the oven to 180°C fan/200°C/400°F/gas mark 6, and find an oven dish that measures 18 x 25cm (7 x 9 inches).

In a medium-size frying pan, heat the oil and fry the red onion until soft and beginning to colour, around 10 minutes. Add the defrosted spinach, paprika and salt, and cook for a couple of minutes until any liquid has evaporated. Allow the mixture to cool, then crumble in the feta and set aside.

Take the pastry out of the fridge, carefully unroll it, place your dish on top and cut around it with a knife, to make a lid. Put the leftover pastry in the fridge or freezer to use another time (e.g. the cheese straws on p. 84).

Scoop the filling into the oven dish and use the back of a spoon to even out the top, then add the pastry on top and use your fingers to crimp the pastry to the edges of the dish. Brush lightly with oil, scatter with the black sesame seeds and bake in the oven for 20–25 minutes until the pastry is golden brown.

TACO BAR

You can double the bean part of this recipe to freeze it – leaving just the rice and garnishes to do at the time.

FEEDS 6

2 tablespoons olive oil
1 onion, peeled and diced
1 teaspoon garlic powder
1 teaspoon cayenne pepper
1 teaspoon ground coriander
1 teaspoon ground cumin
1 x 400g/14oz can kidney beans, drained
1 x 400g/14oz can cannellini beans, drained
1 x 400g/14oz can chopped tomatoes
300g/10½oz brown basmati rice

TO SERVE
160g/5¾oz mangetout, finely shredded
200g/7oz sweetcorn (canned, or frozen and defrosted)
160g/5¾oz Cheddar, grated
Guacamole, optional
1 packet of soft corn tortillas

Preheat the oven to 200ºC fan/220ºC/425ºF/gas mark 7.

To make the beans, heat the oil in a (flameproof) casserole or other heavy-based pan (for which you have a lid) over a medium heat and, when hot, cook the onion until soft and translucent, around 10 minutes. Add the garlic powder, cayenne, coriander and cumin and stir well.

Tip in the drained beans and chopped tomatoes, stir well and bring to the boil. When it comes to the boil, pop a lid on and transfer to the oven for 25–30 minutes, until the mixture has reduced and the beans are very soft.

Cook the rice according to the instructions on p. 27.

Place the beans, rice, mangetout, sweetcorn, cheese, guacamole and tortillas all in separate bowls in the middle of the table and let the children build their own meal.

HEAD CHEF CHARLIE AND SOUS CHEF SARA, STORMONT HOUSE SEN SCHOOL

"Everyone at Stormont House loved Charlie from the beginning. When he smiles, there is such a feeling of warmth that it's contagious. Like many of the team, Charlie wanted to work in school food to make a difference. I knew he would fit in perfectly.

Sara is now Charlie's second-in-command. They are doing extremely important work, helping kids with additional needs to enjoy many different types of food. They encourage them to smell, taste and touch new ingredients, showing how playing with food can be a good thing!

Sara and Charlie remind me of the power that food has to bring people together. When Charlie walks around the canteen, all the kids will call him over and ask about their meal. They want to know everything! But when the food is served up, the room falls silent... everyone eats!" Nicole

SARA'S ETHIOPIAN CHICKEN CASSEROLE

Berbère spice blend is a fragrant mix typical to Ethiopian cuisine containing chilli, black pepper, cumin, coriander, fenugreek, allspice, cloves, ginger, cardamom and nutmeg. With this recipe, you need to allow time for marinating and should ideally begin it the day before you want to serve it.

This recipe is on the following page

SARA'S ETHIOPIAN CHICKEN CASSEROLE

FEEDS 6

600g/1lb 5oz chicken thigh, cut into 3-cm/1-inch pieces

4 tablespoons olive oil

6 garlic cloves, peeled and minced

2 onions, peeled and finely chopped

2 red peppers, cut into 3-cm/1-inch pieces

Small bunch of thyme, leaves picked

2 tablespoons tomato purée

2 tablespoons Berbère spice blend

500g/1lb 2oz chestnut mushrooms, quartered

2 courgettes, cut into 3-cm/1-inch pieces

Sea salt and black pepper

Sliced spring onions and herbs of your choice, to serve

Injera, to serve (see below)

In a medium-size bowl or dish, add the chicken thighs along with 1 tablespoon of the olive oil, 2 of the minced garlic cloves and ½ teaspoon each of salt and pepper. Mix together well, cover and refrigerate, ideally overnight.

When you're ready to cook the stew, heat 2 tablespoons of the oil in a large (flameproof) casserole (for which you have a lid) over a medium heat and sear the marinated chicken until golden. Using a slotted spoon, remove the chicken from the pan and set aside. Add the final tablespoon of oil to the casserole and fry the onion, remaining garlic, red peppers, thyme leaves, tomato purée and Berbère spice blend until soft and caramelised, stirring regularly so that the spices don't burn.

Add the mushrooms and courgettes and return the chicken, along with any resting juices, to the pan and stir well. Pour over 500ml/18fl oz water, stir in ¼ teaspoon salt, bring to a simmer and cover with a lid. Cook on a gentle heat, stirring occasionally, for around 45–50 minutes until the meat is tender and the courgettes have collapsed. Taste for seasoning, scatter over spring onions and herbs of your choice and serve with the injera bread. (Although having the casserole with injera is the traditional way, it can be served with the Jollof on page 102 or the Maltese Potatoes on page 114 – anything to get children to taste different flavours.)

INJERA

Injera is a traditional fermented flatbread that is usually made over the course of three days, which allows for the teff flour to ferment before forming a batter that is similar to a crêpe and pancake but with a spongier texture. However, this recipe uses an active sourdough ferment as an alternative, which means it should only take around 40 minutes to prepare.

FEEDS 6

200g/3½oz bubbling active sourdough starter

200ml/3½fl oz water

1 teaspoon sea salt

In a bowl, whisk together all the ingredients – the consistency of the mix should be thicker than a crêpe batter but thinner than a pancake batter. Once combined, cover and leave for around 30 minutes.

When the batter has rested, place a medium non-stick frying pan (for which you have a lid) over a high heat and, when hot, pour a ladleful of batter into the pan, swirling it to evenly coat in a thin layer. (You do not need to oil the pan.)

Cover the pan with the lid and allow the batter to cook for around 60–90 seconds, or until bubbles form and the outer edges lift away. Slide the injera onto a plate and set aside as you repeat with the rest of the batter.

Serve on a plate, golden side-down, topped with Sara's Ethiopian Chicken Casserole (opposite).

COUSCOUS TABBOULEH

Most kids love couscous, so at school we make tabbouleh with it instead of the more traditional cracked wheat. It also provides a good way into salads.

FEEDS 4

50g/1¾oz couscous
100g/3½oz ripe tomato, finely chopped
100g/3½oz baby cucumber (or any cucumber), finely chopped
1 shallot, finely chopped
Juice of 1 lemon
Sea salt
1 teaspoon allspice
5 tablespoons olive oil
Large bunch of mint, finely chopped
Large bunch of parsley, finely chopped

Place the couscous in a small bowl and pour over boiling water to just above the surface. Cover with a clean tea towel and set aside to rest.

Place the chopped tomato and cucumber in a large bowl (juices and all). Add the shallot, lemon juice and couscous to the bowl, season with salt and then toss to combine.

Whisk the allspice into the oil and drizzle over the couscous. Scatter over the fresh herbs and gently fold in to finish.

TONI'S JOLLOF RICE WITH POT-ROAST CHICKEN

"When I arrived as chef at Gayhurst, the multicultural kitchen were battling to cook British food for a diverse school community. When I suggested the kitchen cook a menu from home, Toni, a school kitchen assistant, made her jollof rice and it went down a storm. It's been on the menu ever since. To make the rice without chicken, simmer on the hob in the sauce (lid on) for 25 minutes." Nicole

FEEDS 6

1 whole chicken (around 1.5kg/ 3lb 5oz)

2 tablespoons olive oil, plus extra for roasting

1 onion, peeled and roughly chopped

2 red peppers, stalk and pith removed, roughly chopped

1 red chilli, seeds removed and roughly chopped (optional)

1 garlic clove, peeled and roughly chopped

2 tablespoons tomato purée

125ml/4fl oz tomato passata

1¼ teaspoons sea salt

400g/14oz basmati rice

Herbs of your choice, to serve

Preheat the oven to 220°C fan/200°C/400°F/gas mark 6. Rub the chicken with a little olive oil and roast for 30 minutes.

Meanwhile, make your jollof sauce. In a large (flameproof) casserole (big enough to fit the whole chicken in and for which you have a lid), heat the 2 tablespoons of olive oil and cook the onion until soft and golden, around 10 minutes.

Add the cooked onions to a large jug along with the peppers, chilli (if using), garlic, tomato purée, passata, salt, and 500ml/ 18fl oz water and, using a stick blender, blitz to a smooth sauce, then set aside.

Wash the rice in cold water until the water runs almost clear. Drain well and add to the large casserole, along with most of the jollof sauce and stir to combine.

After the chicken has been roasting for 30 minutes, take it out of the oven and reduce the temperature to 160°C fan/180°C/350°F/ gas mark 4. Carefully transfer the chicken (it will be very hot!) to the casserole dish and nestle it gently into the rice. Pour the remaining jollof sauce over the top of the chicken, then put the lid on the pot and transfer to the oven.

Cook for 45 minutes, then remove the lid and cook for a further 15 minutes, until the chicken skin is nicely bronzed. Check the chicken is cooked by inserting a sharp knife between the thigh and the breast; the juices should run clear.

Once the chicken is cooked, remove the pot from the oven, take out the chicken and put on a board to rest for 10 minutes before carving. Replace the lid on the rice so it can sit and steam.

Fluff up the rice with a fork, carve the chicken and serve on top of the rice, sprinkled with herbs of your choice.

LAMB KOFTE

We love seeing the kids tuck into this Middle Eastern treat at lunch. We let them eat them with their hands in pittas or on flatbreads.

FEEDS 4-6 (MAKES 10 KOFTE)

500g/1lb 2oz minced lamb
1 tablespoon ground coriander
2 teaspoons cumin seeds
1 teaspoon dried rosemary
½ red chilli, finely chopped
Small bunch of fresh mint, finely chopped
Small bunch of fresh coriander, finely chopped
Sea salt, to taste
Olive oil

CUCUMBER YOGURT
200g/7oz plain yogurt
½ cucumber

TO SERVE
Wholemeal pitta bread or flatbread (p. 122)
Couscous Tabbouleh (p. 101)

In a medium-size bowl, mix together all the ingredients except the olive oil.

In a frying pan, fry a small amount of the mixture to check for seasoning and adjust if necessary. Weigh out the mixture into portions of 50g/1¾oz each, and shape each into a sausage shape around a skewer. Arrange the kofte on a plate and allow them to rest in the fridge for 2 hours.

When you're ready to cook the kofte, preheat the oven to 180ºC fan/200ºC/400ºF/gas mark 6. Heat a little oil in a frying pan and sear the kofte on all sides, then transfer to a baking tray and place in the oven for a further 10 minutes.

To make the cucumber yogurt, grate the cucumber. Squeeze out any water you can with your hands and stir through the yogurt.

Serve with wholemeal pitta bread or flatbrad, couscous tabbouleh and cucumber yogurt.

STAR ANISE BEEF WITH CARROTS AND CHICKPEAS

This stew is wonderfully fragrant and a great way to introduce star anise. It is made to go with the kimchi (p. 119) which cuts through the richness of the meat and adds a fragrant hit of the East.

FEEDS 8

2 large onions, peeled and roughly chopped

2 jalapeño chillies, deseeded and roughly chopped

2 red peppers, roughly chopped

30g/1oz fresh coriander

2 garlic cloves, peeled and roughly chopped

2 teaspoons cinnamon

2 tablespoons smoked paprika

2 teaspoons ground cumin

2 teaspoons dried oregano

1 teaspoon sea salt

4 star anise

500g/1lb 2oz beef shin, diced

4 carrots, peeled and cut into 3-cm/1¼-inch pieces

2 x 400g/14oz can chickpeas, drained

Steamed rice (p.26), to serve

Kimchi (p. 119), to serve

In a large bowl, throw in all the ingredients in the list up to the star anise. Using a stick blender, blitz to a rough paste. Transfer to a container, add the star anise and beef and cover in the marinade. Cover with a lid and refrigerate overnight.

Preheat the oven to 150ºC fan/170ºC/325ºF/gas mark 3. Transfer the beef and its marinade to a small casserole pot, add the carrots and chickpeas and stir to combine. Cover with a lid and cook for 2 hours, until the beef is tender.

Serve with steamed rice and kimchi.

SIDE
S

"I was training at a new school where the kids weren't used to salads on the table. I took sugar snaps, just tossed in olive oil and sea salt, and put them in bowls on the tables. I went and sat on one table with the kids and said, 'Who wants to try one?' and I took a bite. No one wanted to be first. Eventually, one child wanted to have a go. It was like a ripple effect – by the time I got to the end tables, I was like the pied piper. One child, who was overweight, said it was the nicest snack he'd ever had, and that he was going to ask his mum to get them for him. I went back to check on the school a year later – the transformation in the child was amazing. He runs up to get his food and he eats really well. His mum has told the school how grateful she is. Now, when I put a sugar snap in a stir-fry, I know the children will eat it." NERISSA

S AND HARING

Sharing plates may have been done to death by the restaurant world, but at school, they're still a radical new concept. We try to make our food a point of fun and wonder, putting an array of colourful and interesting cooked and raw salads on the tables before children come into the dinner hall. A whole cauliflower roasted in paprika until bronzed and tender, a platter of sweet yellow corn, sharp and fresh in a dressing of lime and honey, and an edible garden of vegetables planted in hummus and olives. There doesn't have to be vast quantities, but it introduces them to a new world of food and allows them to explore it for themselves. Often, it's their first restaurant-type experience and it introduces and enables a new texture or flavour that isn't just dolloped onto the plate.

EDIBLE GARDEN

"The first time Oli and I made the Edible Garden, a Nopi classic, for Gayhurst was just an epic moment for me – educational, beautiful, joyful, with the kids all eating vegetables. It was everything in one moment and I remember thinking that we were on to something here." Nicole.

For this recipe you'll need two small loaf tins or other vessels deep enough to 'plant' the veg into – tumblers or squat mugs also work.

FEEDS 4-6 TO NIBBLE ON

400g/14oz hummus
24 baby vegetables for 'planting'
e.g. radishes, carrots (with leaves
if possible), baby cucumber and
tenderstem broccoli, trimmed and
peeled, with tops on, or cut into
small spears
Flatbread (p. 122), to serve

FOR THE 'BLACK SOIL'
75g/2¾oz stale, good-quality bread
Olive oil
75g/2¾oz black olives, pitted
50g/1¾oz pumpkin seeds
1 teaspoon cumin seeds
Generous pinch of chilli flakes

First make the 'black soil': preheat the oven to 100°C fan/120°C/250°F/gas mark ½. Toss the stale bread in a little olive oil and arrange with the black olives on a baking try to dry out for 4-5 hours.

Place a dry frying pan over a medium heat and toast the seeds and chilli flakes until fragrant. Transfer to a blender with the dried olives and bread and blitz together.

Tip the mixture back onto the baking tray and rub the soil together to feel if it is dry enough. If not, return to the low oven for an hour or until dry.

Divide the hummus between the loaf tins. Scatter over the black soil and plant in the veg. Serve with flatbread.

WHOLE ROASTED CAULIFLOWER

I love the theatre of this dish. We put the golden cauliflowers onto the tables with sharp knives sticking out of them – smaller children are so excited about being allowed to handle a sharp knife (supervised) that they find themselves trying the dish, too.

FEEDS 4

1 cauliflower, left whole, small
    leaves attached
4 tablespoons olive oil
2 tablespoons sweet paprika
½ teaspoon sea salt

TO SERVE
2 tablespoons sesame seeds
2 tablespoons sunflower seeds
3 spring onions, thinly sliced or
    fresh herbs

Preheat the oven to 220°C fan/240°C/475°F/gas mark 9.

Place the cauliflower in a (flameproof) casserole, for which you have a lid.

In a small bowl, mix together the olive oil, paprika and salt and drizzle over the cauliflower. Place the lid on and roast in the oven for 10 minutes, then lower the heat to 190°C fan/210°C/410°F/gas mark 6½ and cook for 10 minutes more, or until a sharp knife inserted into the centre of the cauliflower slides in easily, and it feels tender. Remove the lid and cook for another 10 minutes, until golden on top.

While the cauliflower is roasting, set a small frying pan over a medium heat and toast the seeds until lightly golden.

Transfer the cauliflower to a serving plate, scatter over the spring onion or herbs and seeds, and serve whole at the table.

MALTESE POTATOES

These potatoes – a mixture of melting and crisp – are as delicious for a dinner party as they are for a family meal.

FEEDS 4

Olive oil

4 medium potatoes, thinly sliced

1 onion, peeled and thinly sliced

Sea salt

1 tablespoon fennel seeds

1 tablespoon vegetable stock
   powder

Preheat the oven to 220°C fan/240°C/475°F/gas mark 9. Pour 4 tablespoons of oil into a roasting tray and scatter the potato slices over. Distribute the onion slices on top of the potatoes. Drizzle over more olive oil, season with salt and sprinkle with fennel seeds and the stock powder.

Pour over 4 tablespoons of water and then bake for 40 minutes until the potatoes are golden and tender.

Delicious with Baked Hake (p. 51), Tommi's Chicken Thighs (p. 69) or even just with a fried egg and some Chilli Sauce (p. 29)

CORN SALAD

The sweet-sour flavours of the dressing transform this storecupboard staple, bringing the corn alive.

FEEDS 4

50g/1¾oz unsalted butter

500g/1lb 2oz corn kernels, canned or
   frozen and defrosted (drained
   weight – 3 x 198g/7oz cans)

½ lime, squeezed to get 1 tablespoon
   juice

1 tablespoon honey

1 garlic clove, peeled and grated

¼ teaspoon salt

⅛ teaspoon cayenne pepper

Bunch of coriander, leaves picked,
   to serve

In a large frying pan over a medium heat, melt the butter. When it's foaming, add the corn kernels and cook until they just start to bronze, around 10 minutes.

Meanwhile, place all the remaining ingredients (apart from the coriander) in a large heatproof bowl and stir to mix. When the corn is cooked, tip it into the bowl and stir to coat in the dressing.

Leave to rest and absorb the flavours for at least 30 minutes before serving, topped with the coriander leaves.

RoseMARY BROCcOLI

We love the crispness and flavour that roasting adds to the broccoli here.

FEEDS 4-6

2 heads broccoli, chopped into small florets, stems roughly chopped
1 teaspoon ground cumin
1 teaspoon ground coriander
½ teaspoon sea salt
Bunch of rosemary, leaves picked
2 tablespoons olive oil

Preheat the oven to 220°C fan/240°C/475°F/gas mark 9 and line a large oven tray with a baking mat.

Place the broccoli in a large bowl with the spices, salt, rosemary and olive oil. Using your hands, mix until the broccoli is coated in the oil and seasonings, then tip onto the lined oven tray.

Roast for 7–9 minutes, until the broccoli is beginning to bronze.

KISIR

In Turkish culture, kisir is made with cracked wheat and served as a mezze or appetiser. Pre Covid, we used to make huge pyramids of it and place them in the centre of the table for children to serve themselves, but it is still an excellent recipe to serve from the service counter.

FEEDS 4

1 tablespoon olive oil
1 red onion, finely chopped
2 garlic cloves, peeled and crushed
2 teaspoons ground cumin
1 red chilli, halved, deseeded and finely diced
20g/¾oz tomato purée
500ml/18fl oz Basic Stock (p. 30), boiling hot
250g/9oz couscous (plain or wholegrain)
Juice of 1 lemon
4 plum tomatoes, finely diced
Sea salt and black pepper

Heat the oil in a saucepan (for which you have a lid) and sauté the onion to take off the raw edge. Add the garlic and cook for a few seconds, stirring gently. Add the cumin and chilli and cook for another minute, then stir in the tomato purée. Now add the couscous and hot stock and remove from the heat. Season, then stir everything with a fork. Cover and set aside to sit for about 15 minutes, when all the liquid should have been absorbed.

Fork the grains to separate them, then add the lemon juice and chopped tomatoes and serve.

PAN-FRIED CABBAGE

This cabbage is irresistible – slightly caramelised and very moreish. You can substitute any cabbage for the ones listed: spring green, Savoy, even Brussels sprouts. Combining two varieties adds interest but it's not strictly necessary.

FEEDS 4

1 teaspoon sesame oil

1 teaspoon grated ginger

1 Chinese leaf cabbage, roughly chopped

1 sweetheart cabbage, roughly chopped

1 teaspoon tamarind paste

25g/1oz butter

1 spring onion, trimmed and finely sliced (optional)

1 carrot, peeled and cut into matchsticks (optional)

Bunch of coriander, leaves picked, to serve (optional), or micro herbs

Place a wok or large frying pan over a high heat and add the sesame oil. Fry the ginger for a minute or two, then add your cabbage and keep stirring – you want it to caramelise but not burn. Add the tamarind paste and stir through.

When the cabbage leaves are soft, remove from the heat. Add the butter, and the spring onion and carrot if using, and stir to combine. Cover with a lid and set aside to rest for 10 minutes.

Toss before serving, scattered with coriander, if you like.

GINGER PEAS

Pepping up peas with these flavours transforms this everyday staple, and pan-frying them is much easier and quicker than boiling.

FEEDS 4

2 tablespoons butter

300g/10½oz fresh or frozen and defrosted peas

1 tablespoon grated ginger

1 teaspoon red chilli powder

In a pan or a wok melt 1 tablespoon of the butter and add the peas. Turn the heat or flame to high and let the peas absorb the butter for about a minute. Remove the peas from the pan before they start popping.

Return the pan to the stove and add the remaining butter. Add the grated ginger and chilli and stir-fry for a few seconds, then fold in the peas.

KIMCHI

We put this out as a sharing plate sometimes and dare the children to sniff and have a little nibble of it. It's quite challenging but exciting, too, when they try. If you cannot find Chinese leaf cabbage, you can use a white cabbage instead.

You will need a sterilised jar. To do this, wash the jar well in hot soapy water, then rinse and leave to dry in the oven (100°C fan/120°C/250°F/gas mark ½) for 15 minutes.

MAKES ONE 500G JAR

- 1 Chinese leaf cabbage (about 500g/1lb 2oz), roughly chopped into 5-cm/2-inch square pieces
- 1 tablespoon sea salt
- 2 tablespoons Korean red pepper flakes
- 2-cm/1-inch piece of fresh ginger, peeled and grated
- 1 garlic clove, peeled and grated
- 1 tablespoon ground turmeric

In a large bowl, toss the cabbage with the salt, making sure all the shredded leaves are evenly covered, then set aside for 2 hours or so. After this time, rinse thoroughly in cold water and drain really well.

In a small bowl, mix the red pepper flakes, ginger, garlic and turmeric with 3 tablespoons of water, to form a runny paste.

Place the dry cabbage in a large bowl and mix in the paste, massaging it into each leaf until thoroughly coated.

Press the kimchi into a sterilised jar so that a little liquid rises to the top to cover the cabbage. You need about 2cm/1 inch of space between the liquid and the top of the jar, and it's important that the cabbage is submerged, so top up with a little water if needed.

Cover with the lid but do not fasten it, leave it loose, and keep at room temperature for a day to kickstart the fermentation process. After that, store in the fridge (keeping the lid loose) for up to a month.

The heat and sourness of this makes it perfect with Star Anise Beef (p. 106) or almost any rich savoury dish.

"A rat-a-tat-tat! That's how we teach children to test bread – tapping on the base in time and seeing if it's done. For our cookery classes, soda bread is our favourite loaf and perfect for young chefs. In the school kitchens, the teams get creative. Dough is made from scratch, cheese and herbs might be sprinkled in, seeds added on top, with different glazes, sometimes sourdoughs or flatbreads. Whatever we bake, the school benefits – what better welcome is there than the scent of baking bread wafting through the corridors." TOM WALKER, HEAD FOOD EDUCATOR, HACKNEY SCHOOL OF FOOD

BREAD

Most people don't make their own bread and many never will. But if you don't or you won't or you think you probably can't, you're missing out. The first cookery lesson our Reception classes take is to learn how to make soda bread. Watching them march to the school gate at the end of the day, bearing their loaves aloft with pride, ready to take home and share, is one of the high points of our school year. Making a loaf of bread is one of the simplest, most rewarding activities there is in the kitchen. Here are a few of our favourite basic recipes – go on, have a go.

FLATBREAD

Traditionally, flatbread is a type of bread that is made without yeast and therefore doesn't rise. While it originated in ancient Egypt, many cultures have versions of flatbread – naan in Afghanistan and India, tortilla in Central and South America, piadina in Romagna, Italy – and we've produced flatbread in just about every school we've worked in.

MAKES 10

360g/12½oz spelt flour, plus extra
   for dusting
½ teaspoon baking powder
1 teaspoon sea salt
200ml/7fl oz tepid water
Butter
3 teaspoons olive oil

In a large bowl, mix together all the dry ingredients and make a well in the middle. Pour in the water and start to incorporate it into the flour. When it has come together, tip it out of the bowl onto a dry, clean worktop and knead it until you have a smooth, pliable dough.

Cover and set aside to rest for 15 minutes.

Divide the dough into 10 equal pieces and, using your palm, roll each into a ball. Place these onto a baking sheet, cover, and set aside to rest for another 15 minutes.

On a lightly floured worktop, roll each ball out into a flatbread shape. Place 1 teaspoon of butter in a large frying pan over a high heat and fry each flatbread until golden on both sides. When cooked, wrap in a clean tea towel to keep warm while you fry the others.

BASIC BREAD

This is a great everyday loaf, good for sandwiches and toast, and a lovely mixture of wholemeal and white flour so it doesn't feel too worthy. It's free-form in shape, so you won't need a tin.

MAKES 1 LARGE LOAF

250g/9oz strong white flour, plus extra for dusting

250g/9oz spelt or wholemeal flour

7g/¼oz sachet instant dried yeast

2 teaspoons sea salt

350ml/12fl oz tepid water

A little olive oil

Tip your flour, yeast and salt into a large mixing bowl. Pour in the water and mix to a sticky dough. Lightly flour a large, flat worktop and scoop the dough out onto it. Knead the dough by pushing it flat with your hands, stretching it out and then folding it back on itself, and rotate it 90 degrees each time you do this. After 5–10 minutes of kneading, the dough should have lost its stickiness and become smooth and elastic.

Lightly oil the inside of your bowl, then place the kneaded ball of dough back in, cover with a clean tea towel and place somewhere warm for 1–2 hours, until it doubles in size.

Once doubled, tip the dough out onto a floured surface and knock it back, by squeezing and pushing the air out of it for a couple of minutes. Bring the dough back into a ball by stretching the sides out and tucking them under to form a smooth top – this will be the crust. Dust it heavily with flour, place it back in the bowl, cover with a tea towel and return it to its warm place to rise again for an hour.

Put a deep oven tray filled with water at the bottom of the oven. This will create a steamy atmosphere which helps to create a good crust on your loaf. Preheat your oven to its highest setting, 220°C fan/240°C/475°F/gas mark 9. Your dough should now be about double the size again and will have spread alarmingly (don't worry). Gently tuck it back into a neat ball, being careful not to knock the air out this time and cut a line or a cross through the middle of it with a sharp pair of scissors to allow it to rise.

Lightly dust another oven tray with flour, and carefully transfer your loaf onto it, then put in the oven as quickly as possible so you don't let too much heat out of the oven.

Bake for 10 minutes, then turn the heat down to 200°C fan/ 220°C/425°F/gas mark 7 and cook for a further 25–35 minutes. You can then test for doneness by tapping the bottom of the loaf – it should sound hollow. Leave to cool on a wire rack before slicing into it or you will damage the delicate interior.

SODA BREAD

"Teaching soda bread was the first hands-on class I ever taught to 5-year-olds. Each pupil's face shone with pride as they marched out of the school gates to share their loaves with their families. I have been hooked on the rewards of teaching kids to cook ever since." Nicole

MAKES 1 LARGE LOAF

500g/1lb 2oz spelt flour

1 teaspoon sea salt

2 teaspoons bicarbonate of soda

1 teaspoon any herb, spice or seed
 of your choice (optional)

300ml/10½fl oz buttermilk (see
 below to make your own)

1 tablespoon oats

Preheat the oven to 180°C fan/200°C/400°F/gas mark 6.

In a large bowl, mix together the spelt flour, salt and bicarbonate of soda. Add a teaspoon of your chosen flavouring (I personally like chilli, turmeric, fennel seeds, rosemary or sunflower seeds, but be creative – dried seaweed also works well).

Make a well in the middle and pour in the buttermilk, then stir until the mixture all comes together.

Tip out onto a floured worktop and shape into a ball. Cut a deep cross into the top and sprinkle with oats. Transfer to a baking tray and bake in the oven for 30-40 minutes. To work out if it's cooked, tap on the base – it will sound hollow when done. Cool on a wire rack, then serve.

CHEF'S NOTES

To make your own buttermilk, put 2 tablespoons lemon juice into 300ml/ 10½fl oz full-fat milk, stir and set aside for 10 minutes. This is a really good way to use milk that's just turning a little sour.

TOM'S WHoLEMEAL PIZzA

"Make with kids as they love getting stuck into the dough. In summer, they'll pick the vegetables from the school's garden and happily add them to the toppings. On a rainy day, we cook this on a hob, and on a sunny day we'll use a wood-fired oven or fire up the BBQ. The drama of the fire, the mess of the flour going everywhere, the colours of the toppings – you're smelling smoke, seeing, feeling, tasting and enjoying. The theatre and joy of food is bottled in this simple recipe."
Tom Walker, Lead Chef and Food Educator at the Hackney School of Food

MAKES 4

100g/3½oz strong white flour, plus extra for dusting
100g/3½oz strong wholemeal flour
½ teaspoon sea salt
1g dry active yeast
130ml/4½fl oz tepid water
2 teaspoons extra virgin olive oil, plus extra for drizzling
1 teaspoon onion seeds

In a large bowl, place the flours and salt and mix together. Put the yeast, water and oil into a measuring jug and mix well.

Make a well in the centre of the dry ingredients and gradually pour in the wet mixture, using a fork to combine as you go. Once the dough has come together, tip it onto a floured worktop and knead for approximately 5 minutes until the dough is smooth, tight and springy. Cover with a clean tea towel and set aside to rest for 45 minutes.

Preheat the oven to 220°C fan/240°C/475°F/gas mark 9.

Tip the dough out onto a lightly floured worktop and divide into four equally sized pieces. Either using a rolling pin or by hand, stretch out the dough until about 5mm/¼ inch thick. Place each pizza on a baking tray, sprinkle with the onion seeds and bake for 6–8 minutes or until puffed up and golden. Drizzle with a little more olive oil and serve with the roasted vegetables below.

SCHOOL OF FOOD GARDEN'S ROASTED VEGETABLES

At the School of Food, we cook this dish over a fire pit, but you can use a barbecue. Make sure your coals are white, with no flames.

1 red onion, thickly sliced into 8
12 cherry tomatoes, cut in half
100g/3½oz green beans (green/yellow/purple), topped and tailed
2 courgettes, peeled into long ribbons
½ lemon
pinch of chilli flakes

First prepare the marinade. Place the garlic with the rosemary leaves in a pestle and mortar with a large pinch of sea salt and pound and grind until you have a smooth paste, then pour in the olive oil and mix well. Set aside.

Place all the vegetables in a large bowl and pour over the marinade. Toss to ensure everything is covered, then set aside for 20 minutes to absorb the flavours.

2–3 sprigs of fresh parsley, finely chopped, to garnish
handful of toasted mixed seeds (e.g sunflower, pumpkin, flax), to garnish

FOR THE MARINADE
2 garlic cloves, peeled
large sprig of rosemary, leaves picked
large pinch of sea salt
4 tablespoons extra virgin olive oil

Place each marinated ingredient onto the grill above a hot fire pit and leave to cook and caramelise for 2–3 minutes on each side. Do not move them too often as the vegetables will begin to break apart.

Once the vegetables have softened and browned, return them to the bowl, squeeze over the lemon, sprinkle with chilli flakes and gently mix.

Serve on Tom's Wholemeal Pizzas (opposite) or Flatbread (p.122), garnished with the chopped parsley and toasted seeds.

HELEN, HEAD CHEF, EGA AND GAYHURST

"Helen is the creative genius behind the Golden Custard (see pg. 146). This recipe demonstrates the challenges we face in school food – you want to make a dish that is good for the kids, but also one they will want to eat. When Helen started transforming the food at Elizabeth Garrett Anderson School, the kids were being served powdered custard. This needed to come off the menu as it is against our ethos. Egg-based custards failed miserably. Helen then had the idea for the Golden Custard, which was a hit.

Helen teaches us all about perseverance. Working in school kitchens is challenging. Our ethos of making meals from scratch requires more work from the team. And then there are the children to win over. Helen is now leading the team at Gayhurst, where the Chefs in Schools' vision is old news, but still there are difficult days – perhaps a child who does not want to try something new. When these children come back for seconds, this gives us all hope that more success stories will follow." Nicole

SOUSOU, GAYHURST SOUS CHEF

"SouSou used to help out at Gayhurst when they needed extra staff. When she first came into the kitchen, I realised she was uber-skilled but needed to learn how to go from cooking for four to 500 or 600. We got along well. I'm Maltese and understand a little Arabic but, with food, you can still connect with people without using language by simply working together, making bread together. SouSou ended up being my teacher with bread, saying I didn't have the patience to wait – and I don't.

SouSou taught me patience. My bread skills were basic but I could give her a recipe from any restaurant and it would come out tasting exactly the same. We started doing twirls, garlic bread, tahini breads – all sorts. For Christmas, the expectations were high, so we'd do a massive tahini reel bread with all different seeds. SouSou doesn't even weigh anything; she just knows what to add. She is a Sous Chef now at Gayhurst and very experienced. She's also still telling me to be more patient!" Nicole

SouSou and Helen

SOUSOU'S APRICOT AND DATE LOAF

This dense sticky loaf is similar in consistency to malt loaf and a slice makes a great after-school snack.

SERVES 10

100g/3½oz black treacle
50g/1¾oz butter
1 teaspoon bicarbonate of soda
225g/8oz dates, diced
175g/6oz dried apricots, diced
50g/1¾oz dark brown sugar
2 free-range eggs, beaten
225g/8oz self-raising flour, sifted

Place the black treacle and butter with 150ml/5fl oz water in a saucepan over a medium heat and let it melt. Remove from heat, add the bicarb (expect it to fizz a little) and stir through the dates and apricots. Cover and set aside for 2 hours to allow the fruit to soften and soak up the liquid.

Preheat the oven to 160ºC fan/180ºC/350ºF/gas mark 4. Grease and line a 900g/2lb baking tin.

Stir the brown sugar, beaten egg and sifted flour into the dried fruit mix until everything is combined. Pour the mixture into the tin and bake for 1 hour or until a knife or skewer inserted into the centre comes out clean. Allow to cool for at least 20 minutes before slicing.

BREA
AND

"I used to cook for Buddhist monks. They'd eat their first meal at 8 a.m., after three hours of meditation, and so the warmth and simplicity of that meal – a bowl of steaming rice with vegetables and pickles – meant so much to them. It's a very rewarding meal to cook, too. Having a mindful moment at the start of the day, taking a cup of tea and a moment to sit down and eat something nourishing has become part of the language of our time. Not so for kids, whose days so often start with a rush." NICOLE

KFAST
BRUNCH

Breakfast can be so many different things: a grabbed piece of toast as you run out of the door, or a moment to linger over when the house is quiet and there's no rush. For many, it's their favourite meal – savoury or sweet, it tends to be simple and needs to be satisfying. Ditching sugar-loaded cereals is much easier to do when you have some ideas for what might replace them. Here you'll find a few of our favourites, from a prize-winning porridge to a cute idea for eggs and toast soldiers.

Some days are sluggish and treacly to wade through, others feel like you've lived a whole life in them. You can't predict which way today will go – fuel it wisely.

EGGS FOR BRUNCH

This is somewhere between coddled eggs and a croque monsieur. It's a bit special, as there are different parts to assemble, but it's very delicious and perfect for a lazy weekend morning when you have more time.

FEEDS 4

2 slices of bread
50g/1¾oz unsalted butter
50g/1¾oz finely chopped cooked ham
50g/1¾oz grated Cheddar cheese
4 large free-range eggs
Small bunch of chives, thinly sliced, to garnish

Fill and boil the kettle.

Preheat the grill and place the bread on an oven tray. Lightly toast for 1–2 minutes on each side, then butter the toast and layer with ham and cheese.

Butter 4 ramekins and crack a single egg into each. Place a deep-sided roasting tin on the hob, arrange the ramekins in the tin and carefully pour in boiled water from the kettle, so that it comes to 2cm/1 inch below the top of the ramekins. Turn on the heat and cook for 6 minutes.

When the eggs have cooked for 6 minutes, carefully remove the ramekins from the water and place on the oven tray with the ham and cheese-topped toast. Grill for 2–3 minutes, until the eggs are just set and the cheese is bubbling.

Cut the toast into soldiers and serve with the egg on the side, sprinkled with chives.

HOMEMADE YOGURT WITH FRUIT

Homemade yogurt is milder than bought plain yogurt so you shouldn't need to sweeten it. We have suggested making it in jam jars with lids so that kids can 'grab n go' as they run out the door. To make a plain yogurt, omit the fruit and jam and simply leave in a thermos to culture for 24 hours, then decant into a storage container and keep in the fridge.

FEEDS 4

200g/7oz berries, fresh or frozen and defrosted
4 tablespoons low-sugar jam
500ml/18fl oz milk
2 tablespoons plain yogurt
Granola or muesli and coconut flakes, to serve

If you are using frozen and defrosted berries, strain off the liquid. Divide the fruit between 4 sterilised jam jars, then spread over the jam to form a layer between the fruit and the yogurt.

Warm the milk until nearly boiling and then allow to cool until comfortably warm to the touch, like a hot bath (46°C/114°F is the ideal temperature).

In a bowl, whisk the yogurt with a little of the milk, then add the rest of the milk. Stir to combine, then pour very carefully over the fruit, leaving enough space on top to add granola.

Screw the lids on the jars, wrap in a thick towel and leave overnight somewhere warm like a windowsill above a radiator or even nestled up with a hot water bottle. The next morning, transfer to the fridge until ready to eat. To serve, sprinkle with granola or muesli and some coconut flakes.

CHEF'S NOTES

For kids uncertain about fruity lumps, start the journey to homemade yogurt by blitzing the fruit until smooth with a little honey first. You can then stir it through the yogurt before eating.

RUDE HEALTH FRUITY DATE PORRIDGE

"We're proud partners of Chefs in Schools, who turn the healthy choice into a celebration, not a sacrifice. Their army of passionate, talented chefs use a no-tastebud-left-unturned approach to flavour, which allows the school children they inspire and feed to shine from the inside out.

We like to be bowled over by flavour so that means a no-tastebud-left-unturned approach to breakfasts. With that in mind, meet our award-winning Fruity Date Porridge recipe. The breakfast that eats other breakfasts for breakfast. This recipe won the annual World Porridge Championships in Carrbridge, Scotland. Time to try out the breakfast of champions for yourself."
Eliza, Rude Health

FEEDS 4

75g/2¾oz coarse oatmeal
75g/2¾oz porridge oats
450ml/16fl oz Rude Health Almond
   Drink or milk of choice
A pinch of ground cinnamon,
   to taste
½ apple, coarsely grated
A handful of dates, roughly chopped
A handful of dried apples, roughly
   chopped
A handful of dried apricots, roughly
   chopped
Pinch of sea salt, to serve
Yogurt, coconut yogurt or double
   cream, to serve

Combine the oatmeal and oat flakes together. Heat the milk in your favourite porridge pan, add the oat mix and start to stir. Add the cinnamon, grated apple and most of the chopped fruits (saving a little to sprinkle on the top of each bowl) and bring to a simmer.

Simmer, stirring from time to time, for as long as is necessary until just right – usually about 4–6 minutes. Add extra milk if needed, as the porridge should be thick and creamy but pourable.

Serve, sprinkling some of the reserved dried fruits and a pinch of salt on top. Then pour over as much yogurt or cream as you like.

NERISSA'S NO-WASTE APPLE AND TAHINI BUNS

"We hate waste, it's criminal! I developed these when I was wondering how to use up a box of apples that were a bit wrinkly and past their best. It's a great way to use up odds and ends of milk, or milk that's just on the turn, too. They are a fruity take on a classic Swedish cinnamon bun and perfect as a snack after school too. They went down a storm with the kids!" Nerissa Buckley, School Chef Trainer

MAKES 12 SMALL BUNS

240g/8½oz strong white flour, plus extra for dusting

5g/⅛oz yeast

½ teaspoon salt

140ml/3¾fl oz milk (coconut milk or oat milk for vegan version)

2 tablespoons extra virgin olive oil

½ teaspoon ground cinnamon

40g/1½oz soft brown sugar

1 tablespoon tahini

180g/6½oz apples, peeled and cut into small pieces

1 free-range egg, beaten

First make the dough. Mix together the flour, year and salt in a bowl, or the bowl of a food mixer if you are using one. Warm the milk and oil together until tepid (warm to the touch). Pour into the flour mixture and knead either by hand or with a dough hook for 5 minutes until the dough is smooth and elastic. Cover and set aside to prove for 1 hour.

Lightly dust a clean worktop with flour and roll the dough out into a flat 2-cm/1-inch thick rectangle.

Mix together the cinnamon and sugar. Stir the tahini into the apple. Spread a thin layer of apple mix over all the dough and sprinkle with the cinnamon sugar.

Line a baking tray with baking paper. Roll the dough up tight like a sausage, so that it makes a snail-shell swirl shape on the inside. Cut the sausage into 12 rounds and lay them on their sides on the baking tray. If the filling squidges out, just unroll the individual piece and add a bit more in. Set aside to prove for 20 minutes. Preheat the oven to 170°C fan/190°C/375°F/gas mark 5.

Brush the buns with egg wash (or coconut milk) and bake in the oven for 18–20 minutes until golden. Transfer to a wire rack and cool slightly before serving.

> CHEF'S NOTES
>
> To dial up the nutrients, you can make these with a mix of white and spelt or wholemeal flour, in which case, add an extra 10ml/2 teaspoons of milk or water to the dough.

NOPI'S BEANS

Baked beans are such a school classic but most canned varieties include a lot of sugar. However, not so this recipe, which is sweetened with a little bit of maple syrup and flavoured with delicious spices. Served at Nopi for breakfast, it is one of those dishes that really is adaptable for breakfast, lunch and dinner – brilliant with our Turmeric Fish Fingers on p. 39, or simply on toast, whenever you're hungry.

FEEDS 4

3 tablespoons olive oil
1 medium onion, peeled and finely
   chopped
1 medium carrot, peeled and finely
   chopped
1 stick of celery, finely chopped
1 bay leaf
3 garlic cloves, peeled and finely
   chopped
2 tablespoons tomato purée
1½ teaspoons Dijon mustard
½ teaspoon ground cloves
1½ teaspoons maple syrup
2 x cans borlotti or cannellini beans,
   drained (480g/17oz net weight)
150g/5½oz passata
4 slices freshly made toast, to serve

Warm the oil in a (flameproof) casserole over a medium heat and fry the onion, carrot and celery, stirring, until golden.

Add the bay leaf, garlic and tomato purée and stir to combine. Add the mustard, cloves, maple syrup, beans and passata and stir again.

Add 150ml/5fl oz water and stir, then cover and place in the oven at 160°C fan/180°C/350°F/gas mark 4 for 45 minutes.

Serve on freshly made toast.

CHEF'S NOTES

If you are switching from canned baked beans, try blitzing together the sauce before adding the beans for a more familiar, smooth texture.

OLIVE OIL AND MAPLE GRANOLA

We love this make-your-own granola, which is so simple and radically cuts the cost (as well as the sugar content) to turn a treat into more of an everyday option. This recipe is adapted from Nekisia Davis's olive oil and maple granola, reducing the sugar and salt but losing none of the crunch. While it's great for breakfast with yogurt and fruit (p. 134 if you want to make your own), a grabbed handful makes a perfect snack anytime, too.

MAKES 1 LARGE JAR

100ml/3½fl oz olive oil
100ml/3½fl oz maple syrup
275g/9¾oz rolled oats
120g/4¼oz sunflower seeds
120g/4¼oz pumpkin seeds
120g/4¼oz pecan nuts or almonds
  (or more seeds)

Preheat your oven to 140°C fan/160°C/315°F/gas mark 2½. In a large bowl, beat together the olive oil and maple syrup, then stir in the dry ingredients and mix well until evenly coated.

Tip onto a baking tray and spread out. Bake for 40 minutes, stirring every 10 minutes, until crisp and just golden. Allow to cool fully before storing in an airtight container.

CHEF'S NOTES

For a stronger flavour, use extra virgin olive oil and add a pinch of sea salt.

MAY'S BREAKFAST MUFFINS

Inspired by a recipe of Ruby Tandoh's, these muffins are simple enough to get into the oven on a school morning, ready to thrust into the hand of a teenager as they head out for the bus. We've suggested a small volume, as they're best eaten fresh from the oven. You can prep the wet and the dry ingredients the night before and keep them separately (wet in the fridge) so that in the morning it's just a case of stirring them together and putting them in the oven.

MAKES 6 MUFFINS

50g/1¾oz unsalted butter, melted

1 small ripe banana, roughly mashed

100g/3½oz plain yogurt

1 free-range egg

1 teaspoon baking powder

110g/4oz spelt or wholemeal flour

Pinch of salt

3 tablespoons muscovado or coconut sugar

60g/2¼oz porridge oats

A handful of berries, fresh or frozen and defrosted

Preheat the oven to 180°C fan/200°C/400°F/gas mark 6, and line a muffin tin with muffin cases.

In a large bowl, beat together the wet ingredients (butter, banana, yogurt and egg).

In a separate bowl, sift the baking powder with the flour. Add a pinch of salt and mix in the sugar and porridge oats. Stir in the wet ingredients until just combined, then divide the muffin mixture between the cases and push a few berries into the top of each.

Bake in the oven for 25 minutes, or until risen and springy to the touch.

CHEF'S NOTES

To dial up the nutrients here, replace a tablespoon of flour with ground almonds or add a couple of tablespoons of crunchy peanut butter.

DES

"When I started working at a SEN school, the kids loved their puddings – which were high in sugar and low in nutrients. Gradually, we started adding in fruit and vegetables. Beetroot was not a popular vegetable for a main, let alone for a pudding – until we put it in a brownie. Once the kids were used to the taste of it, we started serving it in other dishes and, finally, in big chunks in salads. Pudding doesn't just have to end a meal, it can be the start of a journey with new ingredients." CHARLIE, HEAD CHEF, STORMONT HOUSE

SERTS

Whether it's a traditional seasonal crumble under a blanket of golden custard, or the dampest of carrot cakes, we really believe in proper pudding, but we don't believe in it every day. For a start, it would be unfair to use up a child's allowance of sweet things at school. To add to that, fruit can go a long way. We try to attach a couple of promises to our puddings – the first is that we use as little refined sugar as possible (if any at all), the second is that there is something positively nourishing in them. Most of our puddings are made with half fruit or vegetables, whether that's under a crumble (such as the one on p. 144) or baked into a cake, such as Nerissa's butternut squash cake on p. 153. Of course, there's the odd exception, such as the tahini brownies on p. 151. But even at school, you occasionally have to break the rules!

FRUIT CRUMBLE

We love the summer strawberry version of this crumble, but you can use any fruit: classic apple, stone fruit such as plums or apricots, and berries, fresh or frozen depending on the time of year. Kale crisps up in the oven and adds a hit of nutrients and an extra dimension of flavour and texture.

FEEDS 4

600g/1lb 5oz fruit, prepared (apples peeled and roughly chopped; stone fruit, pitted and roughly chopped; frozen berries, defrosted)
60g/2¼oz golden caster sugar, or to taste

FOR THE CRUMBLE TOPPING
60g/2¼oz kale
100g/3½oz oats
40g/1½oz pumpkin seeds
20g/¾oz poppy seeds
1 scant teaspoon fennel seeds
Pinch of sea salt
1 teaspoon ground turmeric
40g/1½oz unsalted butter, plus extra for greasing
80g/2¾oz honey

Golden Custard (p. 146), to serve

Preheat the oven to 180°C fan/200°C/400°F/gas mark 6 and grease a 27 x 18cm (11 x 7in) deep-sided oven dish with butter.

Tip the fruit into the oven dish and sprinkle with the sugar. Stir briefly to mix, then bake in the oven for 15–20 minutes until soft and bubbling.

Meanwhile, place the kale in the bowl of a food processor and pulse until blitzed into very small pieces. Add the oats with the pumpkin, poppy and fennel seeds, along with the salt, and pulse to combine. Tip into a bowl, add the turmeric and stir through.

In a small saucepan, melt together the butter and honey. (You could also do this in the microwave.) Once melted, pour in the kale and oat mixture and stir to combine. Sprinkle this topping over the cooked fruit and then return the dish to the oven for a final 15 minutes. The topping should be slightly crisp, but don't cook it for too long or you will lose the vibrant Kermit green of the kale. Serve with Golden Custard.

HELEN's GOLDEN CUSTARD

"I was having a tricky time at a secondary school where the kids weren't adapting too well to the new food. One of the big stand-offs was over custard, which I'd taken off the menu as it was made from a powdered mix. Everyone was asking me when the custard would come back, even the Headteacher. I knew I could win back some support from them if I could recreate the style they were used to. Taking the idea of traditional Ayurvedic 'Golden Milk', I developed this softly spiced yellow custard, which had the added bonus of introducing the kids to a range of spices as well as improving wellbeing. There was a collective sigh of relief when custard made a comeback on the menu – I'm not sure anyone even noticed the difference." Helen Cottle, Head Chef, Gayhurst Community School

MAKES 500ML/18FL OZ

500ml/18fl oz whole milk

1-cm/½-inch piece of fresh ginger, peeled and roughly chopped, or ½ teaspoon ground ginger

2-cm/1-inch piece of fresh turmeric, peeled and roughly chopped, or ½ teaspoon ground turmeric

1 cinnamon stick or 1 pinch ground cinnamon

4 cardamom pods, gently cracked open, or 1 pinch ground cardamom

Pinch of black pepper

1½ tablespoons sugar

2 teaspoons vanilla extract

2 tablespoons cornflour

Heat the milk in a small saucepan set over a medium heat until just below the boil, then remove from the heat and add the ginger, turmeric, cinnamon, cardamom and black pepper. Set aside for 30 minutes, to allow the spices to infuse the milk.

Strain the milk through a sieve, discard the spices and return the milk to the pan. Place it over a medium heat and bring it back to a gentle simmer. Add the sugar and vanilla extract and stir to combine.

Place the cornflour in a small heatproof bowl and pour a few tablespoons of the warm milk over the cornflour. Stir until you have a thin paste, then add this paste to the rest of the milk, stirring all the time to avoid lumps. Bring to the boil briefly until thickened and custardy and serve with Fruit Crumble (p. 144).

HENRY'S UPSIDE-DOWN APPLE AND CARDAMOM TART

"My Mum was brought up in Syria and was always cooking with spices. This was the first pudding I ever made and was inspired by her. It is so simple and delicious and makes me think about her every time I cook it." Henry Dimbleby, Chefs in Schools Co-founder

FEEDS 6

3 cardamom pods
Juice of 1 orange
4 tablespoons soft brown sugar
40g/1½oz unsalted butter
4 apples (about 650g/1lb 7oz), thinly sliced
Flour, for dusting
200g/7oz puff pastry

Preheat the oven to 160°C fan/180°C/350°F/gas mark 4. Crush the cardamom pods and keep the little seeds.

In a saucepan, place the orange juice, sugar, butter and cardamom seeds and simmer until thickened and syrupy. Pour the syrup into a 25-cm/10-inch flan tin (not one with a push-out bottom, or it will seep through and go everywhere). Arrange the apple slices symmetrically on top of the syrup in the flan tin.

Dust a little flour over a clean worktop and roll out your pastry to a size just larger than the flan tin. Carefully lift it up and lay it over the apples in the tin, trimming off the excess around the edges. Sprinkle a little more sugar on top if you like.

Place in the oven for 30 minutes or until the pastry has risen and is golden. Set aside to cool a little.

Place a large serving plate on top of the pastry and, holding on tightly, flip the whole thing over. Tap the bottom of the tin to ensure that all the apple slices are on the plate, then remove the tin and a magically neat and tidy tart will appear. Serve with cream or Golden Custard (see opposite).

CHEF'S NOTES

You can use almost any fruit – pears, plums, apricots, nectarines, peaches and oranges all work well. With oranges, a shortcrust pastry and a really treacly syrup made with molasses as well as sugar works really well.

ON-THE-RUN CEREAL BAR

These cereal bars are enough of a treat to serve as a picnic pudding or snack in the car, yet pack enough nourishment to feel quite wholesome as well. They're flexible friends, too: feel free to use what you have in the pantry. Cornflakes can be swapped for any similar breakfast cereal (preferably low sugar). Raisins can be currants, dates or dried apple, chopped to raisin-size pieces, and the dried apricots could be swapped out for more chocolatey prunes. Honey can also be any syrup: agave or maple both work for less of a sugar-rush.

MAKES 15 BARS

150g/5½oz cornflakes
200g/7oz oats
150g/5½oz raisins
100g/3½oz dark chocolate, roughly chopped into small pieces, plus more for topping (optional)
Pinch of sea salt
100g/3½oz dried apricots
150g/5½oz coconut oil
2½ tablespoons golden caster sugar
1½ tablespoons honey

Line a 20-cm/8-inch square tin with greaseproof paper. Half-fill and boil the kettle.

Tip the cornflakes into a large bowl and scrunch with your hands to break them into smaller pieces. Add the oats, raisins, chocolate and salt and stir to combine.

In a small heatproof bowl, tip in the apricots and pour over enough boiled water to cover them, then set aside to plump up.

In a small saucepan over a medium heat, melt the coconut oil, sugar and honey together until simmering, then take off the heat. Drain the soaked apricots and mix them into the oil and sugar mixture. Using a stick blender, blitz to a smooth paste.

Pour the apricot paste into the bowl of dry ingredients while it's still warm – this will melt the chocolate a little and help stick everything together. Using a large spoon or spatula, mix really well until everything is covered in the apricot mixture, then tip into the lined tin and press down really well with your hands.

Place the tin in the fridge for a couple of hours to allow the mixture to set, before cutting into 15 bars.

CHEF'S NOTES

Stored in an airtight box in the fridge, these bars keep for up to a week – if you can make them last that long.

TAHINI BROWNIES

These are the most delicious brownies that have a dash of extra interest, brought by tahini and halva. They can be served warm and gooey, or cold, when they will set a bit more.

FEEDS 12

180g/6½oz unsalted butter, roughly chopped

180g/6½oz dark chocolate (70–75% cocoa solids), broken into roughly 4-cm/2-inch pieces

3 free-range eggs

150g/5½oz golden caster sugar

90g/3¼oz flour (you can also use gluten-free plain flour)

25g/1oz cocoa powder

Sea salt

110g/3¾oz tahini paste

100g/3½oz halva, broken into 2-cm/1-inch pieces

Heat the oven to 180°C fan/200°C/400°F/gas mark 6, and line a 20-cm/8-inch cake tin with baking paper.

Quarter-fill a small saucepan with water and place over a high heat. Bring to the boil, then reduce the heat to low and sit a heatproof bowl over the pan, making sure its base does not touch the water.

Place the butter and chocolate in the bowl and leave for about 2 minutes to melt. Remove from the heat and stir until you have a thick, shiny sauce. You could also do this in short bursts in the microwave. Set aside to cool down to room temperature.

In a large bowl, whisk the eggs and sugar until pale and creamy and the whisk leaves a trail behind it – about 3 minutes with an electric whisk, longer by hand. Gently fold the cooled chocolate mix into the eggs – do not overwork – and then fold in the flour, cocoa and ½ teaspoon sea salt. Pour into the lined tin and spread out into an even layer.

Use a spoon to dollop the tahini onto the brownie mix in about 12 places, then use the back of a clean spoon to swirl it a little through the mix – not too much; you want it uneven. Dot the halva on the surface, pushing it down a little so that it is well submerged but still visible.

Bake for 12–15 minutes, until the top is crisp and the middle still has a slight wobble. The brownies may seem a bit undercooked at first, but they will firm up as they cool down.

Cut the baked brownie into 12 slices and serve warm-ish (and gooey) or at room temperature (and not quite so gooey).

NERISSA, SCHOOL CHEF TRAINER

"Nerissa was employee number one at Chefs in Schools – but brings the enthusiasm of ten to our charity. Nerissa's joy for food lights up every classroom and kitchen. When things go wrong, she will always have a solution and magic incredible dishes out of few ingredients. Her passion for getting kids to enjoy vegetables knows no bounds. She puts them in cakes, breads, sauces and in snack bowls, always explaining what they are.

Food can be very emotional – when children take that step to try a new ingredient it can be a lovely moment. On occasions, we've had tears in our eyes when a child enjoys a new dish. We've also had a lot of laughs. Nerissa teaches me about determination and enthuses me on difficult days." Nicole

NERISSA'S BUTTERNUT SQUASH CAKE

"This recipe is one we share with every school we work with. It was developed out of necessity but became a hit. I was at a school one day and we needed a cake ASAP for lunch. We like to get as much fruit or vegetables to our cakes as we can and I was hunting around for some to put in, when I remembered we were baking butternut squash whole in the oven for the next day. It was a lightbulb moment and what a yummy result." Nerissa Buckley, School Chef Trainer

This recipe is on the following page

NERISSA'S BUTTERNUT SQUASH CAKE

FEEDS 8

125g/4½oz unsalted butter
125g/4½oz golden caster sugar
2 free-range eggs
200g/7oz cooked butternut squash
250g/9oz self-raising flour
1 teaspoon ground cinnamon
¼ teaspoon ground nutmeg
Edible flowers, to decorate

FOR THE ICING

100g/3½oz unsalted butter, at room
    temperature
100g/3½oz soft light brown sugar
85g/3oz maple syrup
220g/7¾oz cream cheese

Preheat the oven to 180°C fan/200°C/400°F/gas mark 6 and line a 20-cm/8-inch cake tin with reusable baking paper.

In a large bowl, cream the butter and sugar together until light and fluffy. Add the eggs, one at a time, and beat again until pale and creamy.

Add the cooked squash, flour and spices and gently fold in to combine. Pour the mixture into the lined tin and bake for 45 minutes until lightly golden on top and a knife or skewer inserted into the centre comes out clean.

Make the icing while the cake is cooling: beat the butter, sugar and maple syrup (an electric beater makes this easier) until light and airy, then add the cream cheese, a quarter at a time. Continue to beat for about 2 minutes until smooth and thick. When the cake is completely cool, smear all over the top and sides. Decorate with edible flowers.

CHEF'S NOTES

To cook the squash, bake whole in the oven at 220°C fan/240°C/475°F/gas mark 9 for 40 minutes, turning it over halfway through. To reduce waste, instead of discarding the pulp and seeds, you can dry them out in the oven at 150°C fan/170°C/340°F/gas mark 3½ for 1 hour, then blitz them into a powder and add to the cake mix.

We have suggested Ottolenghi's cream cheese icing here, though at school we serve it un-iced.

LUCIE'S CARROT CAKE

This classic is from the 1960s and has been passed down through the kitchen staff at The Totteridge Academy, previously Ravenscroft High School. The recipe they use is from a scanned copy of an old typewritten version! It's an absolute favourite with our students and a healthier option with wholemeal flour, carrot and coconut in there too.

FEEDS 12

140g/5oz brown sugar

100ml/3½fl oz neutral oil, such as sunflower

2 free-range eggs

7g/¼oz baking powder

1 teaspoon ground cinnamon

140g/5oz grated carrot

45g/1½oz desiccated coconut

110g/3¾oz wholemeal flour

Preheat the oven to 160°C fan/180°C/350°F/gas mark 4. Grease and line a 900g/2lb loaf tin.

Mix all your ingredients together in a bowl until incorporated and pour your mixture into the tin. Bake for 25 minutes.

Leave to cool before cutting, and enjoy!

CHOCOLATE BARK

Snacks are always really good to have at hand at the school gate and this recipe is exceptionally easy. You will only need a few shards every afternoon so you can do this recipe once over the weekend and then store and use whenever you wish.

MAKES 6-8 SHARDS

200g/7oz chocolate, dark or milk
Zest of 1 unwaxed orange
Big pinch of sea salt
50g/1¾oz coconut flakes

Line a baking tray with greaseproof paper. Quarter-fill a small saucepan with water and place over a high heat. Bring to the boil, then reduce the heat to low and sit a heatproof bowl over the pan, making sure its base does not touch the water.

Break the chocolate into the bowl and heat until it is almost melted, but not quite – you want a few pieces of solid chocolate to remain. You could also melt the chocolate in short bursts in the microwave.

Remove the bowl from the heat, stir in the orange zest and salt, and give the chocolate a final stir to melt the solid pieces.

Pour the melted chocolate onto the greaseproof paper, using a spatula to spread it out as evenly as possible. Sprinkle over the coconut flakes and allow to set at room temperature. Don't be tempted to speed this up by putting it in the fridge, or the chocolate will bloom (develop unattractive but harmless white patches on the surface).

When the chocolate has set, break into 6–8 shards, and store in an airtight box, at room temperature.

INDEX

US GLOSSARY

Aubergine - eggplant

Baking/cake tin - baking
  pan

Beetroot - beets

Bicarbonate of soda –
  baking soda

Broad beans – fava beans

Caster sugar – superfine
  sugar

Chickpeas – garbanzo
  beans

Chilli – chili

Chinese leaf cabbage –
  napa cabbage

Coriander - cilantro

Cornflour - corn starch

Courgette - zucchini

French beans – fava beans

Frying pan - skillet

Grill – broiler

Kitchen paper – paper towel

Loaf tin – loaf pan

Pepper, red or yellow – bell
  pepper

Plain flour - all-purpose
  flour

Porridge oats – old-
  fashioned rolled oats

Prawns – shrimp

Red pepper – bell pepper

Rocket – arugula

Sieve - strainer

Spring onions – scallions

Tea towel – dish towel

Wholemeal flour –
  wholewheat flour

ACKNOWLEDGEMENTS

NICOLE:
Oliver Pagani – my friend, co-creator. The book, Gayhurst and Chefs in School – all created from a friendship I cherish. Thank you.
Naomi Duncan, and the Chefs in Schools team. I could never have believed we would have such a dream team.
All the chefs who are in schools, believing that this is possible.
Issy Croker and Emily Ezekiel – what is the next one? Thank you!
SouSou and the team at Gayhurst.
Nature's Choice, Fenns of Piccadilly and Bethnal Fish and Brixham, thank you for your patience and for supplying our schools.
And no. 82 Astbury Road for the prawn toast and being great guinea pigs. Hannah – for the patience, patience and more patience.
Jo Weinberg – without us thinking we can better what children ate in schools we would never have got where we are today.
To all our volunteers and supporters, for everything you do to inspire and help us.
Last but not least, Henry and Louise for believing in what can be possible in schools and not questioning it.

JO:
The Chefs in Schools team for making me part of this project; what you do is amazing, I salute you. Danielle, you have contributed so much to this book, from the language to the chefs' stories and more. Hannah Cameron McKenna for your thoughtfulness and attention to detail with the recipes. Tommi for scooping me on to this bus. Henry for teaching me so much. May and Billy for letting me go away to work every week. Kate Schiller for being there for the kids when I wasn't. Sam for the mean read and brilliant support. Katus for mopping up the dark days. Ed for enduring the vats of chickpea chorizo, for the spreadsheets, and everything else, always. Nicole for the laughs, the dreams - and for showing me what's possible with a pancake pan. I love sharing our kitchen with you.

To the Pavilion Team – Sophie Allen for this amazing opportunity to share our mission and recipes, Vicki Murrell and Sarah Epton for editing and proofreading, Nicky Collings for the beautiful design, Komal Patel for spreading the word so enthusiastically and to all the sales team for their energy in helping us achieve lift-off.

OUR FUNDING PARTNERS, PATRONS AND SUPPORTERS
The Fishmongers' Company's Charitable Trust, Mark Leonard Trust, Esmee Fairbairn Foundation, Impact Urban Health, UBS, Ocado, Garfield Weston Foundation, Swire Charitable Trust, Gerald Fox, Arabella Duffield, Belazu Foundation, Kusuma Trust, Rude Health, Hawksmoor, The Food People, James Helm, Issy Croker, Faith Pickin, Indigo Eight and, last but not least, all the individual donors, patrons and supporters. We could not do our work without you – thank you from the bottom of our hearts.

There are lots of people to say thank you to so please excuse us both if your name is not on paper, it will be in our hearts. We are grateful to every person who has contributed to the making of Chefs in Schools from day one.